Lyman Haynes Low

Catalogue Of The Collection Of Copper, Coins And Tokens

Lyman Haynes Low

Catalogue Of The Collection Of Copper, Coins And Tokens

ISBN/EAN: 9783741126666

Manufactured in Europe, USA, Canada, Australia, Japa

Cover: Foto ©Thomas Meinert / pixelio.de

Manufactured and distributed by brebook publishing software
(www.brebook.com)

Lyman Haynes Low

Catalogue Of The Collection Of Copper, Coins And Tokens

AUCTION SALE

OF

Copper Coins and Tokens,

With a few

Medals and Books relating to Coins.

PART II

OF THE COLLECTION OF

COL. WALTER CUTTING,

OF PITTSFIELD, MASS.

On Monday, November 28, 1898,

AT THE COLLECTORS' CLUB,
351 FOURTH AVENUE, NEW YORK CITY.

PART II.

CATALOGUE

OF THE

EXTENSIVE AND VALUABLE COLLECTION

OF

COPPER COINS AND TOKENS,

THE PROPERTY OF

COL. WALTER CUTTING,

OF PITTSFIELD, MASS.,

CONSISTING IN PART OF THE REMAINDER OF THE SERIES OF

ENGLISH TOKENS DESCRIBED BY CONDER,

WITH LARGE AND IMPORTANT REPRESENTATIONS OF

GERMANY, AUSTRIA, ITALY, NAPLES AND SICILY, MEDITERRANEAN ISLANDS, AFRICA, ASIA, (WITH SIBERIA UNSURPASSED IF NOT EVEN UNEQUALLED) AND OCEANICA,

INCLUDING A COLLECTION OF

308 AUSTRALIAN TRADESMEN'S COPPER TOKENS,

ALSO A FEW MEDALS MOSTLY FOUND IN VAN LOON.

CONCLUDING WITH A NUMISMATIC LIBRARY.

———•—

Which will be Sold by Public Auction at

The Rooms of the COLLECTORS' CLUB, 351 Fourth Ave., New York,

HENRY C. MERRY, Auctioneer,

MONDAY, NOVEMBER 28, 1898,

AT TWO O'CLOCK.

———

The Coins will be on Exhibition from 9.30 A. M., to 1 P. M.

———

CATALOGUED BY

LYMAN H. LOW,

UNITED CHARITIES BUILDING, FOURTH AVENUE AND 22d STREET,

NEW YORK, N. Y.

COINS AND MEDALS

(The closing number or that following name of coin)

In this Catalogue, is given in Millimeters.

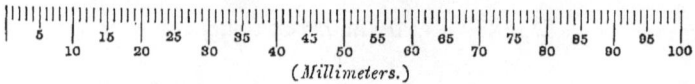

(*Millimeters.*)

ABBREVIATIONS USED.

abt	about.	Ins.	inscription.	S.	Size.
Æ	Copper.	*l.*	left.	S. B.	Small bronze.
Æ	Silver.	Lib.	Liberty.	sep.	separate. separating.
bet.	between.	M. B.	Middle bronze.		
bril.	brilliant.	mil.	military.	std.	seated.
bzd.	bronzed.	*m. m.*	mint mark.	setd.	
Ctms.	Centimes.	mon.	monogram.	shld.	shield.
Ctvs.	Centavos.	mtd.	mounted.	sim.	similar.
CS.	Counterstamped.	n. d.	no date.	sq.	square.
Cwn.	Crown.	O.	Obverse.	stdg.	standing.
cwnd.	crowned.	*Obv.*		supl.	supplement.
d.	Pence.	oct.	octagonal.	sup.	supported.
dbl.	double.	octag.		suptd.	
dif.	different.	pf.	proof.	Trans.	Translation.
do.	ditto.	*r.*	right.	unc.	uncirculated.
Ex.	Exergue.	℞	Reverse.	v.	very.
ex.	extra.	*Rev.*		var.	variety. varieties.
G. B.	Large bronze.	*Res.*	restrike.		
gd.	good.	Rl.	Reals.	W.m.	White metal.
hd.	head.	Rls.		wrth.	wreath.

U. S. Mints are designated as follows: C., Charlotte; C. C., Carson City; D., Dahlonega; O., New Orleans; S., San Francisco; without letter, Philadelphia.

AUTHORITIES QUOTED.

B., Betts, C. Wyllys, American Contemporary Medals; Catalogue No. 4, S. S. & C. Co., L'd, 1892; Fis., Father A. Fischer Cat, by S. S. & C. Co., 1891; Fon., Fonrobert Catalogue; H., Herrera, Spanish Proclamation Medals; M. I., Medallic Ill. British Hist.; V. L., Van Loon, Medallic Hist. of Holland.

Lot 15 is without small eagle's head under bust.

Lot 56, Conder reference, should be pages 268 and 269.

*** All manner of copies and alterations are excluded from my sales.

*** There are no duplicates in any lot unless so mentioned specially or stated to be unassorted.

Copies of this Catalogue, with Two Plates, giving prices realized, neatly executed in red ink, 75 cents.

☞ INSTRUCTIONS TO BIDDERS.

Coins and medals are sold at so much per piece, U. S. proof sets excepted. You cannot bid for one piece in a lot. If a lot contains ten pieces, and you desire to offer $2 for it, make your bid 20c. The auctioneer will accept an advance of 1 cent up to 50c., then 5c. up to $2.50, when 10c. is the limit, up to $10, and thereafter not less than 25c. Hence any bid up to 50c. can be entertained, but after that the bid must be 55c., 60c., and so on. Such offers as 53c., $1.01, and all intermediate figures are unavailable.

CATALOGUE.

CONDER HALFPENNY TOKENS (18th Century).

The Conder references are indicated by figures; the bracketed figure [1] *refers to page, the others to the particular number on the page.*

1 Huddersfield, [181] 9, Hull, 10, [182] 11 to 15, Leeds, 16, 19, [183] 20 to 23. Fine to unc., most of the best.   13

2 Sheffield. [183] 24 to 27. Fine 3, unc. 1.   4

3 Sheffield Constitutional Soc. ℞ Shield ins. BRITAIN, bet. flags of America, Holland, etc., UNITE & BE FREE. [183] 27. About unc., very rare.   1

4 York. West view of cathedral. *Revs.* Queen's Bays, John Howard, and Britannia seated. [184] 31, 32, 33. Unc., one a proof, all very rare.   3

5 — B. Hobson (brass). "Constantine the Great." Female setd, "Eboracum." Latter fine, others unc.   3

6 Cork. Fame flying *l.* (2 var.), [186] 1, 2. Dublin. Camac, Canac, Kamuc, and Kyan Ryan, Roan Rone, etc. [187] 1 to 7, [188] 8, 10, 11, 12, 15, 17. Mostly good to fine, some are rare.   15

7 Others of Dublin. [189] 18, 21 to 24, 27, [190] 28 to 34, 36, [191] 38. Mostly good to fine, some rare.   15

8 Others. [191] 41 to 44, [192] 46 to 49, 51, 52, 53, [193] 54, 55, 56. Very fine to unc., some very uncommon.   14

9 John Brewer, French arms, Dublin. ℞ DEALER | IN · FOREIGN | WINES AND | SPIRITOUS | LIQUORS. [193] 63. Unc., extremely rare.   1

10 Others. Bryen Boiroimhe, etc., [193] 57 to 62. Munster, [195] 1, 2. Mostly fine, 3 unc., 2 rare.   8

11 Cronebane. A Bishop's head in profile, with and without cro-
sier, 1789-94. [196] 1, 3 to 8, [197] 9 to 13, 17 [198] 20, 22,
24. Good to unc., several rare. 15

12 Others, with revs. "Canac Ryan," etc. H. and bugle horn in
shld, Bishop stdg, etc. [197] 17, 18, [198] 21, 25, 27, (John
Wilkison). Two have Bishop with lumpy face and hair. Gd,
fine and unc. (2), all *very* rare. 5

13 **Not local.** St. Andrew, Archery, Askins, THE | CELIBRATED |
VENTRILOQUIST, 1796 (2 var.). [210] 1, 2, 3, 5, 6. V. fine to
unc. (3 of last), all rare, the last 3 especially so. 5

14 Duke of Bedford (2 var.), British. "Lost to Britannia's Hope,"
etc., by *Dassier*. Another, "Heaven restores your King."
Bust of GEORG · III · ET · CHARLOT · etc., *r*. Others *l.*, "Long
may they reign," etc. [210] 7, [211] 8, 14, 15, [212] 23, 24,
[213] 25, 26, 27. Good to unc., mostly uncommon, 2 are
rare. 9

15 Pattern Halfpenny, 1788, by *Droz*. Small eagle's head (?) and
D. F. under bust. ℞ Britannia setd *l.*, spear in *r.* hand, date
in legend. *Ex.* Rudder and palm branches crossed. Ornamented edge. Æ gilt. Very good. [211] 11. Montague 1
and Spink 759. Of the highest rarity. 1

16 Another, from same dies as last. Edge, " Render to Cesar the
things which are Cesar's : ✳ " [121] 12. A bronzed proof,
extremely rare. 1

17 1790 A very sim. bust *r*. *Droz F.* on truncation. ℞ Britannia setd *l.*, her *r.* arm extended, hand pointing ; date in exergue. Æ gilt. Ornamented edge. [212] 16. Extremely
rare. And a bronzed proof with edge lettered, "Render to
Cesar," etc. [212] 17. Rare. 2

18 "He feels the people's wants." Unc. British Commercial
Halfpenny. Bronzed proof. Another, To | comemerate | his
Majesty | viewing, the | Dutch prizes | at the Nore. | Octr.
30 | 1797 Unc. [212] 18, 19, 22. The last 2 very rare. 3

19 "Britannia Rules the Waves," Standard of England, Charlotta
Dei Gratia (Good, v. rare, Æ, traces of gilt). " Rule Britannia." ℞ Deus Nobis, etc. Another, "A way to prevent
knaves getting a trick." Hope with " Success to Trade and
Commerce." [214] 29 to 36. Fine to unc., the last very
rare and in the choicest condition. 8

20 1795-96 Scales, value and weight of bread. Bust of Wm. III, 1688 within wrth, arms above, Halfpenny below, 1795. [215] 37, 38. The first uncommon, the latter extremely rare, both unc. 2

21 AL-FRED, Claudius, Georgivs Triumpho 1783, etc. [215] 39 to 46, [216] 47, 48, 52, 53, 57, 58, 59, [217] 60. The last a bust *l*. ℞ A cwnd harp, without legend or date, and very rare. Fair to v. good. 16

22 A man handcuffed, padlock on his mouth. "A free born Briton of 1796." ℞ Knife, fork and plate padlocked down to a table, "Useless." Another from same obverse die. ℞ "A French Republican." A sailor standing beside anchor. [217] 61, 62. Uncirculated, both uncommonly rare, and none more prized. 2

23 Brunswick, [217] 61 to 66, Ching, Clyde, with river deity, 3 var., Coal Trade, [218] 69, 71 to 75. Fine to unc., some not easily obtained. 10

24 City besieged. ℞ Ships at sea, war trophy below. Collector's Token, man sitting at table spread with coins. ℞ Ass and mule saluting. Another with asses running for Halfpence. W. Cooper, aged 20 years. [218] 70 very rare, [219] 76, 77 rare, 78 very rare. All unc., red. 4

25 Cornwallis, Cornwell, [219] 79, 86, Druid (complete), [220] 84 to 91, the last with "Little Turnstile" rev. Good to unc., mostly fine, some rare. 10

26 Cultivation. Plow and harrow. ℞ Scales. Another, a wheat sheaf. [219] 81, 82. Both in choice condition and very rare. 2

27 Man sitting at table, carving a joint, ENGLISH SLAVERY. ℞ A man setd on the ground, gnawing a bone, FRENCH LIBERTY. [221] 92. Unc., extremely rare. 1

28 Erskine, Erskine and Gibbs, Filtering Stone, John of Gaunt (complete), Gen'l Convenience, Godiva, Gordon. [221] 93 to 96, [222] 103 to 106, [223] 107 to 113. 1 poor, remainder fine to unc., some are rare. 15

29 Fox. ℞ Medallions and tree. Another "Dedicated to collectors." Samuel Garbett, with blank reverse. David Garrick. [221] 97, [222] 98, 101, 102. All uncirculated, and very rare. 4

30 I Promise ⁝ to Pay on ⌐ demand ⌐ twopence fter ⌐ JN.º GRAY | 1758 ℞ In-
cuse of obv., date is faint, otherwise fine. [223] 115.   1

I believe Conder read his date 1788 from a piece perhaps also defective or
weak at that point. I consider this has just claims for a very high degree of
rarity. I find it checked in no other copy of Conder that I have seen.

31 Handel (3 var.), Hands United, Hardy (3 var.), Howard (5 var.).
[224] 116 to 124, [225] 125 to 127. Mostly very fine, some
rare, the last especially so.   12

32 Howe. [225] 128, 130, 131, [226] 132, 133, 134. Mostly very
fine, some very rare reverses.   10

33 Others, with varying busts. *Revs.* Anchor (2) and Britannia
stdg. [226] 140, [227] 141, 142. The last in white metal.
All unc. and very rare.   3

34 Jervis (complete, the 1797 uncirculated and extremely rare),
[227] 143 to 148, Industry (complete), Irish (4 var., 2 *very*
rare), [228] 149 to 154, 155, 157, [229] 158. Good to
unc.   15

35 Irish Halfpenny Token, Associated Irish Miners' Arms, both
unc. and very rare. Kemp, Kirk, Lackington, Low Hall Col-
liery, and Loyal Britons' Lodge (2 var.). [229] 159, 161, 163,
164, 165, [230] 168, 169, 170. Good to unc.   8

36 I PROMISE | TO PAY | ON DEMAND | 2 PENCE | D Mᶜ VICAR ℞
Incuse of obverse. [230] 171. Good. Brass, extremely
rare.   1

37 Masonic (complete), Mighells, Newton, Noted Advocates, three
men hanging on gibbet. ℞ " A way to prevent knaves getting
a trick " (2 from same die, 1 in *brass*). Also, Open book,
" The wrongs of man." [230] 172, [231] 173 to 179. Good
to unc., some are rare.   9

38 Odd Fellows. A weeping and laughing face united (3 var.).
Rob't Orchard, bust *l.* and hd *r.* [231] 180, 181, [232] 182,
183, 184. The last good, remainder unc. ; the last three v.
rare.   5

39 End of Pain. Man hanging on gibbet, church in distance. ℞
A pair of breeches, burning, " May the knave of Jacobin
Clubs never get a trick." Also, Open book, and combusti-
bles labelled Regicide, Robbery, Falsity, etc. [232] 185, 187,
190, [233] 191, 192. Good (1) to unc., none common, most
are rare, the last especially.   5

40 Peace and Plenty, [233] 193 to 198, Pe . Lew and Pellew (both rare), Queen's Bays, [234] 205, 206, Reform (3 var.). Good to unc., some rare. 13

41 " R. Hon. W. Pitt," bust *l.*, head facing. " J. Priestly, citizen of the world," and " Rev'd W. Romaine." [234] 202, 203, [235] 212. A very rare trio. Priestly fine, others unc. 3

42 Revolution, Roe, Scotland "Gulielmus Vallas," Seymour, Shakespear (8 var.). [235] 210, 211, 213, [236] 214, 215, 217, 219 to 223, [237] 224, 226. Mostly good to fine. 13

43 "Am I not a man and a brother " (3 var.), Stanhope, Sussex, Tom Tackle, John Horne Tooke, Trade. [237] 229 to 232, [238] 233, 236, 237 to 240, [239] 241. Good to v. fine, some scarce. 11

44 Isaac Suainson. Head *l.* ℞ Hygieia preparing Velno's Vegetable Syrup. [238] 234. Bronzed proof, extremely rare. 1

45 Prince of Wales. Bust *l.* (2 var.), facing (4 var.), bust *r.* (5 var.). [239] 243, 244, 246, 247, 248, [240] 249 to 253, 255. Mostly good to fine, some rare. 11

46 Prince and Princess of Wales (brass, good, very rare), Princess of Wales (4 var.), Wilkinson (7 var.), Wilkenson, Wilkison, and Williams. [240] 256, 257, [241] 258, 259, 261, 265, [242] 266 to 271, 273, 274, 275, [243] 276. Mostly very good, some very rare. 16

47 Washingt(on), 1795, Liberty and Sec(urity). Letters enclosed do not show, otherwise good. [241] 262. 1

48 IOHN WILKINSON IRON MASTER. Bust *r.* ℞ FINE SILVER A brig sailing *l.* *Ex.* 1788. Edge, Willey — Snedshill — Bersham — Bradley. In *silver*. [241] 264. Fine and extremely rare. 1

49 Duke of York (complete). [243] 278 to 285, [244] 286 to 289. The first and last have bust *l.*, the remainder with bust *r.* The last " A Member of the Britᵗʰ Senate 1797 " and v. rare. Mostly fine. 12

VARIETIES. ALL RARE, MANY EXTREMELY SO.

50 St. Albans, Anchor (2 var.), Anglesey. [264] 3, 10, 11, [265] 12. All unc. 4

51 Antelope (3 var., one with Louis Rex on rev.), Arms, Skidmore 123 High Holborn. [265] 13, 14, 17, 18. V. fine and unc. 4

52 Ass (complete), An ass loaded with two pair of panniers, " I
    was an ass to bear the first pair," " Rouse Britannia," " After
    the Revolution," Lion dismayed. [266] 22, 23, 24. Unc.   3
53 — A man handcuffed and ironed, padlock on his mouth. An
    American Indian. Boy on turnstile, another turning it. [266]
    25, 26, 27. Unc.   3
54 Aylesbury. ℞ Bust of Howe. A different obv. ℞ Shepherd.
    [267] 31, 35. Unc.   2
55 Bedel. Perspective view, and James Metcalf with rev. St. Paul's
    Covent Garden. Another, with Arms. [268] 41, 43, 44. Unc.   3
56 Birmingham. ℞ A way to prevent knaves, etc. Bridewell Boy.
    ℞ Mendoza. British Liberty, sailor seizing a landsman.
    [368] 45, [369] 49, 50. Fine and unc.   3
57 Sailor as last. Revs. Shepherd, Heart on open book, Lion
    dismayed. [269] 51, 52, 53. Unc.   3
58 — Other revs. The head of a man and ass joined, Armed Cit-
    izens, Cain killing Abel. [269] 54, 55, [270] 56. Unc.   3
59 — Others. ℞ After the Revolution, A free-born Englishman,
    An American Indian. [270] 57, 58, 59. Very fine (1) and
    unc.   3
60 — Others. ℞ Caduceus, Two men boxing, and Little Turn-
    stile. [270] 60, 61, 62. Unc.   3
61 Cambridge. Hood, Print Seller, differing revs. (2). Coaly
    Tyne. ℞ Shepherd, Hand, Highlander, etc. [270] 63, 64,
    [271] 67, 68, 69, 70. Unc.   6
62 Coining Press. ℞ Highlander, Men boxing, Cwnd harp. [271]
    71, 72, 73. Unc.   3
63 Sr. Geo. Cook. Man stdg, smoking. ℞ Man setd gnawing
    a bone (very rare), Cow with two heads, a Toucan on tree.
    [273] 74, 75, 76. V. fine and unc.   3
64 Dog. "Much gratitude brings servitude." ℞ Cain and Abel,
    After the Revolution, and the padlocked Englishman. [272]
    77, 78, 79. Unc. (2), the other fine.   3
65 — Others. ℞ Highlander, Caduceus, and Little Turnstile.
    [272] 80, 81, 82.   3
66 Druid. ℞ P. M. Co., Arms, Anchor and Liberty cap, and
    Sheaf of wheat. [273] 83 to 86. Unc.   4
67 Dublin. Prince of Wales' crest, Fame flying, Arms, Robert
    Orchard. [273] 88, 89, 90, 91. Unc.   4

68 Others. ℞ Hood, Print seller. Another, H in script and bugle
horn in shld. *Revs.* H. S. & Co., Fame flying, Rob't Orchard
and a crown. [274] 94 to 98. Unc.   5
69 Dudley Token. *Revs.* Noted Advocates, Hand, Armed Citizens,
Highlander. [274] 101, 102, [275] 106, 108. Unc.   4
70 Others. ℞ Caduceus, Little Turnstile, Dunmow. *Revs.* Bust
of Garrick and "Mur'd by the factious," etc. [275] 109, 111,
113, 114. Unc.   4
71 Elephant. ℞ Royal male tiger. English Slavery, man sitting
at table, carving. *Revs.* Anchor, Sheaf of wheat between
doves, and a smaller sheaf without doves. [276] 116 to 119.
Unc.   4
72 Fame flying. *Revs.* Wheat sheafs as last, Arms. Foundry.
Men working at forge. *Revs.* Hand, and W. G. M. [276]
122, 123, 124, [277] 129, 130. Fine to unc.   5
73 Bust of C. J. Fox (complete). *Revs.* Spence, Shepherd, Lion
dismayed, Odd Fellows, etc. [277] 131 to 134, [278] 135 to
139. Fine to unc.   9
74 France. Hds of King and Queen. *Revs.* Anchor, Fire grate,
and bust of Garrick. French Liberty, man setd gnawing bone.
Revs. Two wheat sheaves, and cart unloading to vessel at pier.
[278] 141, 142, 144, [279] 145, 147, 148. Unc.   6
75 David Garrick. Gordon (complete), bust *l.* *Revs.* Spence's
Card, Hand, Britannia. [279] 150 to 153. Fine to unc.   4
76 — Others of Gordon. Cain and Abel, Caduceus, After the
Revolution, and Little Turnstile. [279] 154, [280] 155 to
157. Unc.   4
77 William Hallan, Birm. *Revs.* Bust of Garrick, Fire grate, and
bust of Geo. III, "Long live the King." [280] 159 (rare),
160, 161. Unc. (2) and a bronzed proof.   3
78 Hendon Church. *Revs.* Garrick, Dunmore Arms, CHURCH AND
KING, with bust of Geo. III. [281] 164, 165, 166 (edge en-
grailed). V. fine and unc.   3
79 — Others. J. M. O. script, Odd Fellows (planchet cracked),
Holt, Spa House. *Revs.* Beggar, and 10 line inscription.
[281] 167, 170, 171, 172. V. fine and unc.   4
80 Hope stdg holds anchor and quadrant. *Revs.* Wheat sheaf, and
J. E. & Co. script, " Hyde Park " a man skating. [281] 173,
[282] 177, [283] 186. Unc.   3

81   Howe. "May the French ever know Howe to rule the main."
Bust. *Revs.* Bust of Garrick, a fire grate, and G. B. script.
[282] 182, 184, 185. All unc.   3

82   Irish. Arms both sides, man weaving, and another with script
monograms on obv. and rev. [283] 189, 190, 192. All unc.   3

83   Kidderminster. A wool pack. ℞ King and Queen of France.
King of England (complete), bust of George III, *r.* *Revs.*
Wheat sheaf, and 10 line inscription. [283] 194, 195, 196.
All unc.   3

84   Others. King of England. *Revs.* Plow, Scales (2 var.). [284]
197, 198, 199. All unc.   3

85   Others. *Revs.* Beggar, Scales, Fame, and Spa House. [284]
200 to 203. All unc.   4

86   London. Anchor, and King of Munster, Sr. Geo. Cook, and
Loyal Britons' Lodge. *Revs.* Wheat sheaf, and Arms. [284]
206, [285] 208, 212, 213. All unc.   4

87   Marine Boy. *Revs.* Sailor, and Little Turnstile. Mendoza.
℞ Shepherd reclining. [285] 215, 216, 217. All unc.   3

88   Meymott. ℞ Wheat sheaf. Munster. *Revs.* P. of W. crest,
and J. E. & Co. [286] 211, 221, 224. All unc.   3

89   Others of Munster. *Revs.* Arms (2 var.), man weaving, and
bust of Rob't Orchard. [286] 225 to 228. All unc.   4

90   Odd Fellows. *Revs.* Spence's card, shepherd, lion dismayed,
and Armed citizens. [287] 230 to 233. All unc.   4

91   — Others. *Revs.* Cain and Abel, Highlander, Caduceus, and
Little Turnstile. [287] 234, 235, 236, 238. All unc.   4

92   Oppression (complete). Two men dancing around a fire. *Revs.*
Spence's card, Shepherd, Heart and hand. [287] 239, [288]
240, 241. Unc.   3

93   — Others. *Revs.* Britannia, Armed citizens, and After the
Revolution. [288] 242, 243, 244. Unc.   3

94   — Others. *Revs.* American Indian (brass, planchet cracked),
Caduceus (cracked planchet), and Little Turnstile. [288] 245,
246, 247.   3

95   Robert Orchard, bust *left.* *Revs.* Anchor, J. E. & Co. script.
End of Pain. ℞ Little Turnstile. [288] 248, [289] 253,
255. Unc.   3

96   Pandora's Breeches. A pair of breeches on fire. *Revs.* Anchor, Mendoza, Shakespear. [289] 256, 258, 259. Unc.   3

97 Pandora's Breeches. Others. *Revs*. Struck | in honor and |
to perpetuate | the memory of | Shakespeare | etc. Pig.
Revs. Shepherd, Heart and hand, Britannia. [289] 260,
[290] 261, 262, 263. Unc.   4
98 Plough. *Revs*. Beggar, and 10 line ins. Revolution (before),
a man sitting in a prison gnawing a bone (complete). *Revs*.
Shepherd, and Lion dismayed. [290] 265 to 268. Unc.   4
99 Others. *Revs*. Armed citizens, Odd Fellows, Britannia. [290]
269, [291] 270, 271. Unc.   3
100 Others. ℞ A guillotine. Revolution (after). Three men
dancing around a tree. *Revs*. Spence's card, and Stag.
[291] 272, 273, 274. Unc.   3
101 Rhinoceros *r*. *Revs*. Royal male tiger, Elephant. [291] 276,
277. Unc.   2
102 Salisbury. Bust *l*. *Revs*. I. M. O., and a church in ruins.
[291] 278, [292] 280. Unc.   2
103 Sailor (complete). A sailor stdg. *Revs*. Anchor, Spence's
card, Shepherd, and Heart and hand. [292] 281 to 284.
Unc.   4
104 — Others. *Revs*. Lion dismayed, Odd Fellows, Armed citizens, and After the Revolution. [292] 285 to 288. Uncirculated.   4
105 — Others. *Revs*. Highlander, Cat, Britannia, and Pandora's
breeches. [292] 289, [293] 290, 291, 292. Unc.   4
106 — Others. ℞ Little Turnstile. A sailor, smoking. *Revs*.
Spence's card, and Anchor. [293] 293, 294, 295. Unc.   3
107 Scales (complete), 3½ lbs. *Revs*. Spa House, Plow, Beggar.
and 10 line ins. [293] 296 to 299. Unc.   4
108 — Others. ℞ Scales. Another obv. with different scales,
6½ lbs. *Revs*. Spa House, Plow, and Beggar. [293] 300,
[294] 301 to 303. Unc.   4
109 — Others. *Revs*. 10 line ins. Scales ("the sale of corn by
weight"), same with *revs*. A beggar and 10 line ins. [294]
304 to 307.   4
110 Shakespear. Bust *l*. *Revs*. Spence's card, Little Turnstile.
Shepherd. ℞ Stag. [294] 308, 309, 310. Unc.   3
111 Ship (complete). *Revs*. Beggar, 10 line ins. Scales, 3½
lbs., do. 6½ lbs., Plow, and Wheat sheaf. [294] 310 to 312,
[295] 313 to 317. Unc.   7

112 Skidmore. Fire grate. *Revs.* Bust, and Flitch of bacon, Anchor. [295] 318 to 320. Unc.   3
113 Snail and tree. *Revs.* Spence's card, and Stag. Spaniard. ℞ Little Turnstile. [295] 321 to 323. V. fine and unc.   3
114 Spence, his head in profile *l.* *Revs.* His card (2 var.), Shepherd, Heart and hand, Odd Fellows. [296] 324, 326 to 328. V. fine and unc.   5
115 — Others. *Revs.* Britannia, Armed citizens, Lion dismayed, Cain and Abel, and After the Revolution. [296] 330 to 334. Unc.   5
116 — Others. *Revs.* Highlander, Caduceus, Cat, Soldier and citizens shaking hands, and Little Turnstile. [296] 335, [297] 336 to 339. Unc.   5
117 John Thelwall, bust in profile *r.* *Revs.* Spence's card, Sessions House, A free-born Englishman, Liberty cap on pole, Snail, and Little Turnstile. [297], 340, 341, 343, 344, 346, [298] 347. V. fine and unc.   6
118 Horne Tooke, Esq., bust *r.* *Revs.* Spence's card, Bust "Long live the King," Odd Fellows, Armed citizens, Pandora's breeches, and Little Turnstile. [298] 348, 350 to 352, 354, 355. V. fine to unc.   6
119 Tree of Liberty. Four men dancing around pole. *Revs.* Spence's card, Shepherd, Heart and hand, Lion dismayed, Odd Fellows, and Britannia. [298] 356, 357, [299] 358 to 361. V. fine and unc.   6
120 — Others. *Revs.* Cain and Abel, After the Rev., Highlander, Caduceus, Guillotine, Dunmore arms, and Little Turnstile. [299] 362, 363, 365 to 369. Very fine to uncirculated, most of last.   7
121 Truth. Minerva stdg. ℞ Spence's card, 3 fleurs-de-lis, 1790. [300] 370, 372, 373. V. fine to unc.   3
122 A Turk stdg. ℞ Little Turnstile (complete), boy sitting on turnstile, his playmate turning it. *Revs.* Spence, Stag and tree, Anchor, Mendoza. [300] 374 to 378. Very fine and unc.   5
123 — Others. *Revs.* Struck in honor, etc., Coaly Tyne. United Token, laur. head. ℞ Highlander. Westminster Scholar. *Revs.* A Blue Coat Boy, and Little Turnstile. [300] 379, 380, [301] 381, 387, 388. V. fine and unc.   5

124 View of a deserted village (complete). *Revs.* Shepherd, Britannia, Cain and Abel, American Indian, and Highlander. [301] 382 to 386. Fine to unc.   5
125 Wearmouth Bridge, [301] 389. Woodford. ℞ Man weaving. [302] 400. Unc.   2
126 Wheat sheaf. *Revs.* King Wm., H. L. & Co., Arms. A different wheat sheaf, Relief against monopoly. ℞ A beggar. [302] 390 to 392. V. fine and unc.   4
127 — Others. *Revs.* To the Illustrious, etc., Scales (3 var.). Wheat sheaf bet. doves. ℞ London arms. [302] 395 to 399. V. fine to unc.   5
128 **Appendix.** Anglesey, [310] *19, *23, [311] *32 (plain edge), *51 (℞ 1791 not 1797). Dundee, *6. Very fine to uncirculated.   5
129 Plymouth, Blandford, Burnt Island, Southampton, Liverpool. [312] *5, 1, [313] 1, *28. Fine to unc., most of best.   5
130 Perth, Boscabel, with bust of Chas. II, Yorkshire, head *r.* ℞ B. S. Co. [316] *1, *2, [318] *6. Unc.   3
131 Crewkerne, [316] *58, Yeovil, [317] *60, Dublin, [319] *21, Cronebane, *1, Cornwallis, *79, Howe, *141, and Jervis, *148, all [321]. Good to fine.   7
132 GEORGIUS III . D . G . REX ✦ —— ... SOHO ... incuse on a raised border. Head *r.* ℞ ✦ BRITANNIA ◄ also incuse on raised border. Britannia seated *l.*, right arm extended, and hand pointing. Exergue, 1795. Edge plain. Bronzed proof, size 32. A very rare Pattern. [320] *17.   1

HALFPENNIES NOT FOUND IN CONDER.

133 Arnold Works, 1791 (6d), Birmingham Poor House, 1796 (in brass), also C. P. in script, 1797, "Birmingham Halfpenny — for Exchange" in raised letters on raised border. Fine to proof, last 2 very rare.   3
134 Bristol Volunteer Token, 1798, Brunswick, Camac (brass) and Camak, Clerkenwell Foundry Scene. *Revs.* David Garrick, and Metcalf, Bedal. Good to unc., 3 of last.   6
135 Coventry. *Revs.* Gaunt and Cross, Glasgow, Duke of York, 1795. ℞ 1797. Louis XVI and M. Ant., Geo. P. of W., Gaunt, I. M. Co. script (Irish, 3 var.). Fair to fine.   10

136 John Hancock, Umbrella Maker and Coin Dealer. John
Howard. ℞ Lib. & Commerce (T. A. & L. rev.). Leeds,
1793 (2, one has plain edge and is uncirculated), Liverpool
(2). Fair to fine.   6

137 London, Mail Coach, Macclesfield, Pantheon, Odd Fellows,
Montrose (2 var.), Newgate (Æ gilt), Swords, West Cowes,
Peace and Plenty. Good to very fine.   10

138 Norwich. Loyal Military Ass'n, 1797. Sise Lane 1795 (in
white metal). T. Spence. ℞ "When this you see," etc.,
Anchor. V. fine and unc.   3

139 John Thelwall. ℞ Minerva (white metal), Tamworth, Church
and Castle, Southampton (with plain edge), also Mendoza
head and Spaniard stdg, with incuse impressions on rev. V.
fine to unc.   5

140 An original impression of Milton's unfinished Ayrshire for
Col. Fullarton. Head *r.* (of Adam Smith,) without legend.
℞ Female seated. Unc., v. rare.   1

FARTHINGS.

With few exceptions all are rare.

141 Anglesey. Druid's head. ℞ P. M. Co., 1788, '89, '91. [8]
60, [9] 61, 62, 63. Unc. and proof.   4

142 Dundee. M. & Co., a pair of scales. ℞ Sentinel between
cannon and fort. Proof. Horse and cart, 1796. About
uncirculated. Another, same type, 1797. Uncirculated.
[13] 13, 14, 16.   3

143 Macclesfield. R. & Co., bee-hive, 1789. Bust of Chas. Roe,
1790, '92. [25] 20, 21, 23. Unc.   3

144 Cumberland | Lake Token, 1796. [27] 1. Exeter. Bishop
Blaze, 1791, '92 (2). Unc. and proof.   4

145 Poole, 1795, [31] 7. "Essex Token, 1796," compasses, saw,
etc.; Leigh, J. Hemmin Leigh, 1796, [35] 12, 13. Chelten-
ham. Geo. III, 1788 (brass), [39] 15. Unc.   4

146 Portsea Half Halfpenny, 1791 ; Southampton, St. Bevois, 1790,
[44] 33, 34. Lancaster, John of Gaunt, 1791, '92, [61] 49,
50. V. fine 1, unc. 3.   4

147 Liverpool, Ship, 1791, '92 ; Rochdale, 1791, '92, Fleece. ℞
Man weaving. [61] 51 to 54. V. fine to unc.   4

148 Glasgow. Jas. Angus, 1780; Alex'r Hamilton, 1791, [62] 6, 7. Edinburgh. St. Andrew, 1791 (2). Gd, fine and proof. [67] 25, 26.   4

149 Edinburgh. "Picken Fish Tacksman" (poor, but excessively rare). Farthing, 1795. A thistle. Unc. Thomson's Warehouse (in *copper*). Good. [67] 27, 28, 31.   3

150 London & Middlesex, 1793, Geo. and Carolina, Pidcock's, Paroquet and dbl-headed cow. Spence's. ℞ A pig, also Adam and Eve on bank of flowers. [114] 357, 358, 365, [115] 366, 368, 369. Fine to unc.   6

151 — JULIOUS CEASER, 1795, his head *l.* ℞ Payable | in . London | Liverpool | or . Bath . | Unc. Harrison, "Bleeding & Tooth Drawing," 1797. V. good. [114] 359, 364.   2

152 — Denton, Dealer in Coins, "We three block heads be," Crown, Ship and Sir Jeffery Dunstan, all 1795. [114] 360 to 363. Proof 1, unc. 3.   4

153 — Skidmore's. Two men working at a forge, 1795, [115] 367. "Newcastle — Farthing," a sailor stdg, [123] 5. Unc.   2

154 St. David's, 1793, [126] 1. Shrewsbury, a wool pack, 1793, [128] 5. Bath (complete), [137] 61, [138] 62 to 66. Fine 2, unc. 6.   8

155 Litchfield. "Payable on | Whit-Monday | at the | Greenhill | Bank." Stafford. Lion and four castles. [140] 8, 10. Unc.   2

156 Lambeth. Wheat sheaf, 1796; Remains of an ancient Fortress. Both with Denton's card on rev. [150] 24, 25. Unc.   2

157 North and So. Wales (complete), [159] 45 to 51. Mostly very fine.   7

158 Birmingham. "Gen'l Elliot," John Howard, Lutwyche's Press. Stratford. Bust of Shakespear *r.* [174] 129 to 132. Dudley. Thos. Jones, 1796. [179] 16. Unc., all partly bright.   5

159 Dublin. Turner Camac, 1792. Good. T. O. Bryen, Church St., 1790; Canister bet. sugar loaves; Cash bet. bottle and glass. Unc. [194] 64, 66, 67, 68.   4

160 — W. Murphy, Wood St., 1796, same design as Bryen in last lot. David Garrick, Esq. [194] 69 to 72. Unc.   4

161 Not local. St. Andrew, 1792. *Revs.* "Farthing Youngest Son of Fortune," (barely fair, but very rare), also Anchor and cable. Adm'l Lord Bridport. *Revs.* Naval crown, Anchor and cable. [245] 1 to 4. V. fine to unc.   4

162 British. George Rules, 1793 and n.d. [245] 6 to 9. Poor
     and fair. God Save the King. *Revs.* "May a flowing
     trade," etc., and Stork. [246] 11, 12. Unc.   6

163 Geo. III and Charlotte. ℞ Peace and harmony. Sim. ℞
     Patrons of Virtue, 1790 (brass), both *very* choice. Another
     with 2 hearts on rev., also the Soho mint Farthing, 1797,
     both very good. [246] 14 to 17.   4

164 King mtd on bull having ass's head. *Revs.* Thos. Spence, etc.,
     Man walking on his hands and feet, "If the law requires it,
     we will walk thus," Lord Camden. [246] 18, [247] 19, 20.
     V. fine to about unc.   3

165 A cat, "In society live free like me," 1795. Copper Co. *Revs.*
     Stork, and "May a flowing trade," etc., Coronet above 2
     sceptres H — H. [247] 21 to 24. Fine to unc.   4

166 Druid. *Revs.* G. R., 1793, very fine; Hibernia, uncirculated;
     Duncan, fair; A deformed man, uncirculated; Flynn, Grocer,
     and George Gordon, both good. [247] 25 to 27, [248] 28,
     31, 32.   6

167 "Even Fellow," Man and devil's head united. *Revs.* Mum, a
     padlock (brass), Man and ass's head united, George Hair,
     Grocer. [248] 29, 30, 33. V. fine to unc.   3

168 Hibernia. ℞ P. S. Co. Adm'l Lord Hood. *Revs.* Naval
     Crown. Anchor. [248] 34, 36, [249] 37. Unc.   3

169 Adm'l Earl Howe. *Revs.* Man-of-war sailing *l.*, good; sailing
     r., unc.; Naval crown (2 var.), also anchor, v. fine and unc.;
     Glorious Howe, poor. [249] 38 to 42, 44.   6

170 Adm'l Sr. Jno. Jervis. *Revs.* Naval crown, and Anchor. Bee-
     hive. *Revs.* Druid's head, 1795, Dr. Sam'l Johnson. [249]
     45, 46, [250] 38, 49. All about unc.   4

171 Admiral Augustus Keppel. Bust facing. ℞ Man-of-war firing
     guns, above, Victory. [250] 50. Good.   1

172 Admiral Macbride. *Revs.* Naval crown, and Anchor, Robert
     Orchard, bust *l.* [250] 51, 52, [251] 65. Unc.   3

173 Sr. Isaac Newton, head in profile, various, 1771–97. [250] 55,
     [251] 56 to 63. 3 unc., others poor to good.   9

174 End of pain. Man hanging on gibbet. *Revs.* Pair of
     breeches on fire, May the knave of Jacobin, etc., and An
     open book, "The wrongs of man." [251] 66, [252] 67, 68.
     Unc.   3

175 End of pain. Others. *Revs.* Sword and palm branch crossed (small pin hole), "Dealer . in . Coins . Medals," arms in shield. A different man and gibbet, above, P — T. ℞ "Such is the reward of Traitors, 1796." [252] 70, 71, 74. V. fine and unc.   3

176 May Peace be established (2 var.), Revolution, Wm. III, 1688, Æ silvered. Slave, "Am I not a man and a brother." ℞ Man walking on his hands and feet, T. Spence. [252] 72, 73, 75, [253] 76, 77. Good to unc.   5

177 "The three Thomas's, 1796. Three men hanging on a gibbet. Prince of Wales. ℞ The Prince's crest ; a different crest. ℞ A crown. [253] 78 to 80. Unc.   3

178 Prince and Princess of Wales. *Revs.* A boar, "May the Union," etc., 1795. Duke of York. ℞ Farthing, 1756 (not 1796, as in Conder). [253] 81, 82, 83. Good to v. fine.   3

179 **Varieties.** Anglesey. Two men working at forge, 1795. Blockheads. Two heads in profile, vis-a-vis, "We three blockheads." ℞ Dunstan. An open book. *Revs.* P. M. Co., and Hibernia. [303] 401, 404 to 406. Unc.   4

180 Pandora's breeches. ℞ P. M. Co., 1788. Britannia. *Revs.* Thos. Spence, etc., Adam and Eve, and Coaly Tyne, 1796. [303] 408, [304] 410 to 412. Unc.   4

181 Rouse Britannia. *Revs.* "Even Fellows," Man walking on his hands and feet. Bull. *Revs.* Adam and Eve, Coaly Tyne (Æ gilt), and head of T. Spence. [304] 413, 415 to 417, [305] 419. Unc.   5

182 Sir Jeffery Dunstan. *Revs.* Denton Engraver, etc., a cwn, Britannia setd *l.*, and Ship lying at quay. [305] 421 to 424. Unc.   4

183 Odd Fellows. The hds of a man and ass joined. *Revs.* Thos. Spence, etc., Adam and Eve, and Head of Spence. Rob't Orchard, his head in profile, 1796. [305] 425 to 428. Unc.   4

184 Rob't Orchard, as last. ℞ Hibernia, Padlock "Mum," 1796. Pig. *Revs.* Coaly Tyne (Æ gilt), "Even Fellows." [305] 429, [306] 432 to 434. Unc.   4

185 Pig. ℞ Head of Spence. P — T Man hanging on gibbet. *Revs.* P. M. Co., "Even Fellows." "End of Pain." ℞ A Druid's head. [306] 435, 437, 439, [307] 440. Unc.   4

186 Slave, "Am I not a man and a brother." *Revs.* Thos. Spence, Adam and Eve. Coaly Tyne. [307] 441 to 443. Abt unc.   3

187 Others. *Revs.* Head of Spence, and " Even Fellows " (Æ gilt).
Three Thomases, 1796. Three men hanging on gibbet.
[307] 444 to 446. Unc.   3

188 **Appendix.** Ralph Erskin & Co., Glasgow, 1781 Perth, Ancient Tower, Vessels at quay, South Wales 1793, Worcester
1788, and Max Hutton 101 James's St. [314] *6, [316] 6,
[317] *51, [318] 17, [322] *44. Good to v. fine.   5

189 Others not in Conder, including Jacks " Coffee House 3d."
(possibly a later period), also Geo. Randolph & Co., 1799,
and various of Pidcock's, etc., 5 are dated 1801. Mostly
very fine.   12

190 Duplicates of Farthings, including Druid's head, 1791, No. and
So. Wales, with 3 of later period (1 dated 1817), 2 duplicates. Good to unc.   14

190a *Pennies of the later Period,* continued by *Atkins.* 1799 New-
market Penny. Race under saddles. 1800 Diva Britanniæ,
etc. Female head *l.* ℞ " Utile Dulci." The work | of |
John | Gregory Hancock | aged | nine years, etc. " For Ex-
change." Both unc., and very rare.   2

190b 1800 Enniscorthy (2 var.), C(hrist's) H(ospital) 2 var. of
Penny. 1801 Stafford, Penny. Pidcock's, the Cockatoo
and Wanderow. 1802 Pantheon. 1803 Stafford Penny.
Good.   9

190c Others. Beverly Brotherly Soc'y. ℞ JOHN GOULD | FATHER.
Duke of Northumberland, crescent within garter. ℞ The |
boundaries | of | Hareshaw | Common | etc. Perambulated
19th Sept. 1836. Both about unc., partly bright. John
Delaporte | St. Martin's Lane | Charing Cross. Holed
through centre, otherwise good. Sizes 37, 38.   3

GERMANY, HUNGARY, BOHEMIA AND AUSTRIA.

191 Aachen. 1597 6 Heller, CS. with city arms. Poor, but rare.
4 Heller, (16)54-1793 (9), 12 do., 1721-97. Mostly fair to
good.   18

192 Anhalt-Bernberg. 1 Pfg. 1746-1840 (15), 3 do., 1753, 1840
(2), 4 do., 1822, '23 (2). — Dessau. 1861-67 (4), Bear
walking on wall, script monogram and arms. — Zerbst.
1766 1 Pfg. Also an octagonal Tax Token, 1680. Size 30,
fine, others fair to fine.   25

193 Augsburg. 1551 to 1805 $\frac{1}{210}$th Gulden, $\frac{1}{2}$ Krz., Heller, 1 and 2 Pfg, including 5 early Tokens. Fair to good. 37

194 Austria. 1749–1800 Heller, $\frac{1}{4}$, $\frac{1}{2}$, 1, 3 and 6 Krzs. All with bust, excepting 3. Mostly good to fine, many large. 49

195 1807–64 $\frac{1}{4}$, $\frac{1}{2}$, $\frac{5}{10}$, 1, 2, 3, 4, 15 and 30 Krzr. Various coinages, mints and dates. Mostly good to fine, a number unc., many large. 63

196 Baden. 1766–1871 $\frac{1}{4}$ (1), $\frac{1}{2}$ and 1 Krzr. Arms and busts. Many good to fine, some unc. 65

197 Bamberg. 1761–86 Heller (4), Pfg, $\frac{1}{2}$ Krzr. Barby. 1621 3 Pfg. Bocholt. 1762 21 Heller. Fair to v. good. 8

198 Bavaria. Max. I, 4 Heller, n.d., 1 Krzr., 1622, Ferd. Maria, 1671, also Brewery Tokens, 1652 with C. P., and 1680 C. W. P. M., both have beer barrel device. 1810 Max. Jos. Visit to Paris Mint. Good to fine. 15 to 27$\frac{1}{2}$. 7

199 1762–1806 1 Heller (4), 1 Krzr (2), 1 Pfg (26), 2 do. (9). All arms cwnd excepting 5. Good to fine. 41

200 1807–35 1 Heller (14), 1 Pfg (24), 2 do. (14). A variety of designs. Good to fine. 52

201 1839–71 1 Heller (8), $\frac{1}{2}$ Krzr (4), 1 Pfg (18), 2 do. (12). Good to unc. 42

202 Brandenburg. 1752–1811 1, 3 Pfg, $\frac{1}{2}$, 1 Gros. and Schil. All but 3 have F. R. in script. Also a Jeton (15)91. Mostly good. 24

203 Brandenburg-Anspach and Bayreuth. (1620) 1699–1816 1 and 4 Heller, $\frac{1}{4}$ Stbr, 1, 2, 3 and 6 Pfg. Also $\frac{1}{12}$ Thlr, on planchet 27 x 29, corner broken to outer circle. Good to fine. 27

204 Bremen. 1720–1866 1 Schwaren (10), 2$\frac{1}{2}$ do. (7). Also Pattern by *Wilkens*. Arms suptd. *Ex*. S. M. ℞ 1 | S. M. Unc. 30. Good to fine. 19

205 Breslau. 1645 in frame above W(ratislau) cwnd, 3 Groschen CS. A(rmen) S(pital). Fine. 31 x 31. 1

206 AS | 1663 *incuse* stamp in oval. ℞ CS. in relief, 17 W 17 cwnd. Good. Octagon, 28. 1

207 Brunswick-Luneburg, Fred. Ulrich. 1621 3 Flittern. Horse above helmet (5 var.), Lion *r.* (3 var.). Same series, n.d. 1 Flitter. Horse and helmet, 3 do., Lion *r.* and *l.* (3), VI do., Leopards. Good to fine. 15

208 Geo. Wm., 1 Pfg, horse *l.*, 1689–1703. GW, letters linked, 1, 1½ Pfg, 1691–96. Geo. Louis, G. R. in letters, 1, 1½ Pfg, 1717–18. St. Andrew, 1 do., 1726. Geo. Aug., St. And., 1 do., 1728–32. Wildman, tree *right*, 1737–59 (10), tree *l.*, 1737–60 (10). Mostly very good.   33

209 G. R. script, 1, 1½ Pfennigs, 1734–59. George III. 1 do. Wildman, 1763–1804, tree *r.* (9), tree *l.* (12). Mostly very good.   30

210 G. R. script, 1, 1½, 2, 4 Pfg, 1762–1806. St. And., 1 do., 1780-89, 4 do., 1792, '94. Mostly v. good.   38

211 1799 GEORGIVS. P. S. S. C. D. date in legend. ℞ BR. L. PR. E REC. etc. Four armorial shields in cross form. Size 20, 28. Another, sim., GEORGIVS. G. P. S. S. C. D. ℞ REGNI SCOTIAE etc. Size 25. Patterns by *Milton*, in perfect condition, dark olive, very rare.   3

212 Hanover. 1.5.4.6 Brewery House Token. A rooster, B. H. T. ℞ Plain. Very good. 29. Another, n.d. Lion on beer mug (about 1837). Good. 20.   2

213 G. R. script, date on obv., 1 Pfg, 1814, 2 do., 1817, '18. Geo. IV, 1, 2, 4 Pfgs, 1821–30. Wm. IV, 1, 2 do., W. R. R. script and arms, 1831–37. Mostly good to fine.   38

214 Ernest Aug., E. A. R. script, 1 Pfg, 1838–51 (17, including GLUCK | AUF.), 2 do., 1838–51. Geo. V, G. R. script, 1, 2 do., 1852–63. Good to unc.   44

215 Brunswick-Wolfenbuttel. Ant. Ulrich, 1 Pfg, 1710, '14. Aug. Wm., 1 do., 1722–30, all with horse. Lud. Rudolp., 1 do., 1733, L. C., script. Chas., 1, 1½ do., 1737–79, with horse. 1758 Denier for use bet. soldiers and people. Mostly very good, some fine.   28

216 Chas. Wm. Ferd., 1 Pfg, with horse, 1782–1806 (24). Wildman, 1780–88, tree *r.* and *l.* Good, some fine.   32

217 Fred. Wm., 1 Pfg, horse, 2 do., F. W. Chas. 1, 2 do., 1816-30, with horse, and to end of series. Wm., 1, 2 do., 1831–60. Mostly good to fine.   35

217a Buchhorn. Uniface Heller, n.d. Burgau. Heller (2), ¼ Krzr (3), ½ do. (1), 1 do. (6). Camenz. 1622 1 and 2 Pfg. Chur-Pfalz. 1622 Krzr, 1766 Pfg, also ¼ Krzr (4), ½ do (3), 1773–86. Cleves. Wm., 1582 Jeton, 1753 ¼ Stbr. Good to fine.   25

5 217b Cologne. ¼ Stubers, 1736–67, all with script *mon.* (12).
The city, 4 Heller, 1768–92 (5), and Bread Pfg, n.d.,
also a Cooper's Token, 1713 (size 30). Constance. 1772
Krzr. Corvey. 1704–87 2 Pfg (3), 4 do. (1). Good to fine. 24

// 218 Curland. 1762 Solidus. Dantzic. Solidus and Schil., 1801–
12. Dortmund. ¼ Stuber, 1752–56. Eger. 1743 3 Krzr
(in lead). Eichstadt. John Chris., 1612–36 Krzr, n.d. (3
var.). Good to fine, some uncommon, others rare. 14

d 219 Eimbec. 1 Pfg, n.d., Gothic E. Elberfeld. 1817 and 1847
Tokens for 1 Loaf of Bread by the city. Flsenburger.
Tokens for 1 Krzr (2 var.), ¼ and 1 Florin. The last in
iron. Good to fine. 11

/ℎ 220 Frankfort a/m. 1 Pfennig, 1773–1863, 2 do., 1795. Good
to unc. 50

⟶ 221 — Jeton of the Old Soc'y, 1777. Pipes crossed above cup and
saucer. Gate Tokens, A. T., F. T. and E. T. Einlass, also
lead impression of obv. of 2 Pfg. Good to fine, all uncommon. 20 to 28. 5

222 — Jews' Pfgs, 1807–22, Atribuo, Halbag, Theller, etc. 1 poor,
others good to fine. 8

/ 223 Fugger. N F in *mon.*, 1622 ₁⁄₁₂₀, ₈⁄₈ (2) Gulden, M Q F
linked, ₈⁄₈ do., n.d. Fulda. 1769 1 Pfg. Furstenwalde.
F. W., n.d. Galicia. 1774 Schil. Good to fine. 7

⟩ 224 German Empire. 1 and 2 Pfgs, 1873–76, with various Mint
letters on obv., from A–A to J–J. Mostly fine. Also set of
1, 2 (Æ), 5, 10, 20 (N.) Pfgs, 1876–89, in mint state. 31

⌣ 225 Goslar. Leichter Pfg. Goslar. St. M. and Pfgs, 1734–64
(17). Gottingen. ₁₆⁄₂₁ and 1621 4 Pfgs. Haag. 1766 ½
Krzr. Hamburg. Gate Token, 1698, also Jacobi's Music
Hall, swan in oval CS. Good to fine. 22

⟨ 226 Hameln. 1636 1 Pfg. Hamm. 3 Pfg, 1696–1739 (8), 4 do.,
earlier, n.d. Harz. "Glvck Avf." Henneberg. Heller,
1676, '93, '94. Fair to good. 14

/ 227 Hamburg. Water Token. Obv. A cask. ℞ URIN | ZEICHEN |
1697. Fine. 28. Heinrichstadt. Large Token, n.d., plain
reverse, "Commis . Vnd . Lonzeichn . Fine. 50 x 52. 2

𝒪 228 Hesse-Cassel. Chas. Landgrave, 1 Heller, 1724, Lion ; 1725,
'29, Monogram, 4 do., 1726, '28, with head *r*. Good, 1 with
portrait v. fine. 7

229 Hesse-Cassel. Fred. I (King of Sweden), 1 Heller, F R in *mon.*, 1730–47 (13), same in script *mon.*, 1744–50 (6), 1½ do., 1746, 2 do., two Fs back to back, 3 do., with head *r.*, 1735, '40, '48. Mostly good to fine.   28

230 — Wm. VIII, W. L. Z. H., 1 Heller, 1751–57 (8), 2 do., 1752–58 (5), 3 do., with bust, 1755, also W L in *mon.*, etc. Good to fine.   16

231 — Fred II, 1760–85 Guter Pfgs and 1, 2, 3, 4, 6 and 8 Heller. Monograms and arms, includes several of the largest German coins, also a miniature of the 8 Heller, size 7½. Mostly gd to fine.   22

232 — Wm. IX, 1785–1821 1, 2, 3 and 4 Heller. *Mons.* WL and WK, also arms. Good to fine.   24

233 — Later issues, 1822–66 1, 2, 3 Heller, ¼, ½, 1 Krzr. Various types. Many very fine.   73

234 — Darmstadt. 1723–1872 Heller, 1, 2, 3, 4 and 6 Pfgs. Various types, initials and inscriptions, H. D —, G. H. S. M —, G. H. K. M. Mostly very good.   47

235 — Hanau-Müntzenburg, 1 Heller, 1739-73 (6), 2 do., 1745, 1 Krzr, 1773. The last is rare ; good to fine.   8

236 Hervord. 1670 6 and 12 (2) Heller. Hildesheim. Grain Tokens, 1626 (brass), 1629 (square), 1658 (2), 1762, '72 1 Pfg, also Pfgs by the Bishops, 1693–1786 (4). Gd to fine.   13

237 Hohenzollern. Krzrs, 1842, fair ; '52, unc., dif. types. Holstein-Gottorp. ₁½ Schil., 1706. Holstein-Pinneberg. 6 Pfg, n.d. Hoxter. Arms only. Hückeswagner. 1848/49 Bread Token for the Poor. Fair to fine.   7

238 Hungary. Bela IV and Stephen V, 1235–70. St. Maria. R℣ The Kings setd. Fine. 28.   1

239 Others. 1704-1882 Poltura, Gieschel, Kreutzer, etc., including a duplicate of Bela and Stephen, concave, fine, remainder largely good to fine.   26

240 1849 3 Krzr. R℣ Három | Krajczár. Unc., red. 33.   1

241 Isny. Heller, 1695 and n.d. Jever. Heller, 1764, ¼ Stuber, 1799 (the latter under Russia). Kempten. Krzr, 1622. Fair to good, none common.   5

242 Julich and Berg. Chas. Theod., ¼ Stbr, 1765–98 (8), ½ do., 1766-94 (6). Max. Jos., ½ do., 1802, '03, '04, also 3 do. (7), the last issued as base, now appearing like copper. Good. 24

243 Kosfeld. 1694–1763 2, 4 (2) and 8 Pfgs. Lauenburg. ½
Dreilings, 1739 monogram, 1740 horse. Leipzic. Early
with blank *revs.* (2). Liegnitz. 1622 3 Heller. Mostly
good, some rare.   10

244 Lend. 1663–1726 I, IIII and X Heller ? (4). Leopoldstadt.
1704 L cwnd, one with blank rev., 1705 10 Poltura, and 5
do. ? uniface and n.d., both with LS linked. None common,
last 4 rare ; good.   8

245 Liege. Mereaux of the Chapter, 1686–1700 (1 lead). Limb.
and Breitenbach, 1788. Jerstadt. Token for a half day's
personal service. Size 33. Lindau, Heller, n.d. Good,
none common.   6

246 Lippe-Detmold. 1724–1858 and some without date, Heller, 1,
2 and 3 Pfgs, 1 with *mon.*, others a blooming rose. Good
to fine.   28

247 Lothringen. Jetons of Anton, 1508–44, Chas. III, 1560, also
one of Chas. of Steyermark, 1569, all with arms. Good to
fine, scarce.   3

248 Lowenstein-Wert. 1 Pfg, 1765–1804 (16), 1766 2 do., arms
and monograms. Good to fine.   17

249 Lubeck. 1649 Communion Token in lead. Luneburg. 1621
4 Pfg. Magdeburg. 1553 3 Flitter. Mansfeld. 1621, '22
Varieties of the 3 Pfg (6), arms without inscrip. or legend.
Marsberg. 1638 1 Pfg. Mostly very good, uncommon to
rare.   10

250 Mecklenburg-Gustrow. 1589 Scharf. — Schwerin. 1704 1½
Pfg. Others, 1, 2, 3, 5 Pfg, 1831–72. Good to uncircu-
lateo.   19

251 Mecklenburg-Strelitz. 1747–1872 1½, 2, 3, 5 Pfg, Face of a
steer, A F and F W cwnd, also G in German text. Good to
fine.   18

252 Mentz. 1558 ½ and 1 Krzr, arms and date only, with blank
revs. Very rare. Also Gate Tokens for 1 Krzr (oval), 2
do. oblong oct., 26 x 37. Fine, rare.   4

253 — Others. Gate Tokens for 1 and 2 Krzr (1 holed), also a
dupl. of oval in last lot. Fair to good.   4

254 Heller, 1757–1810 (7), 1 Pfg, 1759–82 (6), 2 do., 1759, '60, 3
do., 1760, '61 (6 var.), 4 do., 1766, ½ and 1 Krzr, 1795, '96,
arms, busts and monograms. Good to fine.   24

255 Mettin. Benedictine Abbey in Bavaria, Medalet against Sor-
cery (see Anthon cat., lot 2314, where 15 lines are devoted to
description and history). Minden. Chris., 1599–1633 3
Pfg. Munster. Ertel's Pattern, 1833. Muhlhauser. 2 Pfg,
1737, '67. Good to fine.   5

255a Munich. 1701 C. W — P. M., crowned arms. ℞ Cask bet.
grain stalks. V. good. 21 x 21. 1766 Another, with arms,
cask, letters and date on obv. ℞ Blank. V. fine. Oval,
21 x 24.   2

256 Munster. The Chapter, 1608 3 Schillings. Horse and rider
l., CS. EVB (Ernst von Brabeck). Good, rare. 34.   1

257 — 1608 6 and 12 Pfg, St. Paul on throne. V. good and extremely fine, both CS. Also a Token for the Poor, 1699.
Fine, all rare. 24 to 29.   3

258 — 1661–1714 1, 2, 3 and 4 Pfg, St. Paul stdg. Also 1 and 2
Pfg, 1790, inscriptions only. Good to fine.   16

259 — 1740-90 1, 2, 3, 4 and 6 Pfg, Half length fig. of St. Paul.
Good to fine.   20

260 — The Bishops, Fred. Chris., Fran. Arnold, and Clem.
Aug., 3 and 4 Pfgs, all with script *mon.*, 1703–55 (19).
The City, 1, 1½, 2, 3 Pfg, 1602–1758 (8). Arms. Good to
fine.   27

261 Nassau. Heller, 1842, ¼ Krzr, 1808–22 (11), ½ do., 1813, 1
do., 1808–63 (19), 1 Pfg, 1859, '60. Includes at least 7 coinages. Good to fine.   34

262 Nassau-Orange. N O in script *mon.*, 1 and 2 Heller, 1766,
'91 (4). Nuremburg. 1622 ¾ Guld., 1 Krzr, etc., including V(nter) G(ericht) Token. Good to fine, some very uncommon.   8

263 Nuremburg. 1744 Gulden of 80 Krzrs. Arms in 3 shields,
beneath L O (Losungsamt). ℞ EIN | GANZERBVRGER | GVL-
DEN | 80 KRZ | 1744. Fine, rare. 38.   1

264 Oldenburg. 1802-69 ¼, ½ Groat, 1 and 3 Schwaren. Also
Oldenb.-Birkenfeld. 2 Pfg, 1848. Arms and monograms.
Good to fine.   26

265 Osnabruck. The City, 1726–1805 1½, 2, 3, 5 Pfg. Fair to gd.
(10). Paderborn. The Bishops, Ferd., 1676 to Wm. Anton,
1767 1, 2, 3, 4, 6 Pfg. The City, 3 and 4 Pfg, 1605, '22
(14). Mostly good to fine.   24

266 Parchim, n.d., Petau, 1769. Pfalz-Neuburg, Wolfg. Wm., ¼
Krzr and 1/120 Guld. Pfalz-Zweibrücken, 1764, '67 ¼ Krzr.
Pomerania, 1806 3 Pfg. Posen, 1 Groschen, 1816, '17. Fair
to fine.   9

267 Prussia. A. Mint (Berlin) 1 Pfg, 1821–73, lacking 16 dates.
Good to unc., 16 of the best.   37

268 — A. Mint 2 Pfg, 1821–70, varying dates. Good to unc.   35

269 — A. Mint 3 Pfg, 1821–73, varying dates. Mostly fine, some
unc.   36

270 — A. Mint 4 Pfg, 1821–67. Good to v. fine.   12

271 B. Mint (Hanover) 1867–73 (13), C. Mint (Frankfort a/m)
1867–73 (11), D. Mint (Düsseldorf) 1823–48 (11), 1 to 4 Pfg,
excepting Hanover. Mostly good to unc. Also a 2 Ctm of
Belgium, CS. with Prussian arms.   36

272 Pyrmont. 1761 1, 2, 3 Pfg. Ratisbon. 1549 4 Krzr, 1763 1
and 4 do. Large coins, size 29 ; also finely executed Token,
1673, "Stattgerecht," Justice stdg ; Heller, 1622 and n.d.,
1753–71 (5 octag.), and a small Token, CS. with keys, V–B.
Ravensburg. 1621 XII Heller, arms ; 1655 XII do., a dif.
type and CS. Good to fine, several rare.   17

273 Reuss. Old and young house. Reuss-Gera-Schleitz and Lo-
benstein. ½ Pfg (3), 1 do. (16), 2 do. (1), 3 do. (24). Gd
to fine.   45

274 Rheda. 1659 4 Pfg. Rega. Schilling, n.d. (base). Ritberg.
1703 1 Pfg. Salzburg. 1 Pfg, 1775–1802 (10), 2 do., 1777,
'82, '86, 1 Krzr, 1802, '05, arms, 1 with bust. Good to
fine.   18

275 Rostock. 1 Pfg, 1682–1848 (30), 3 do., 1622–1864 (29), 6 do.,
1761, many varieties of type. Good to fine.   60

276 Saxony. 1582 Jeton, 1624 Rechen Pfg and a Bracteate (size
13). Fine. 16 to 27.   3

277 — The Kingdom, Heller, 1779–1813 (10), 1 Pfg, 1792–1872
(33), 2 do., 1841–73 (16), 3 do., 1811–37 (4), 4 do., 1808, '09,
5 do., 1862–69 (6). Good to uncirculated, several bright
red.   71

278 Saxe-Altenburg. 1 Pfg, 1842, '53, '63, 2 do., 1852. Fine.
— Coburg. Heller, 1682–93 and n.d. (5). Good. V. KR :
and ∗ XV ∗ | KR, cwnd arms, for 5 and 15 Krzr, n.d. Rare.
Size 25, 24. Fine and good.   11

279   Saxe-Altenburg. Coburg-Gotha. 1 Pfg (5), 1½ do. (2), 2 do.
(7), 1835-70. — Coburg-Meiningen. ¼ Krzr, ½ do. (2), 1
do. (2), 1 Pfg (2), 1814-23. Good to fine.   21

280   — Coburg-Saalfeld. Heller (16), ½ Pfg, 1 do. (12), 1½ do., 2
do. (3), 3 do. (9), 4 do. (2), 1699-1826. Mostly gd to fine.   44

281   — Gotha and Altenburg. Heller (8), 1 Pfg (2), 1½ do. (6), 3
do., 1696-1761 (17). — Hildberghausen. Heller, 1703-
1824, a few with letters and monograms, one CS. with a
rooster, but mostly arms (24). V. fair to good, some fine.   41

282   — Meiningen. Heller (3), ⅛ Krzr, ¼ do. (3), ½ do. (5), 1 do.
(8), 1 Pfg (7), 2 do. (8), 1625-1869. Good to fine.   35

283   — Weimar. With S. E. O., Heller (2), 1 Pfg (7), 1½ do.,
1722-55, all with *mon.* (10). With S. W. E., 1 Pfg (4), 1½
do. (2), 2 do. (4), 3 do. (4), 1821-65, arms (14). With S.
W.e.E., Heller (7), 1 Pfg (6), 1½ do. (2), 2 do. (5), 3 do.
(4), 4 do. (2), 1700-1813, arms (26). Fair to fine.   50

284   Sayn-Wittgenstein. ¼ Stuber, 1752-57 (4). Schaumburg.
Wm. IV, 6 Pfg, n.d. Schaumburg-Hessen. 1775-1803,
Guter Pfgs (8), W-L and F-L. Others, similar, 1804-32
with W-K (21). Schaumburg-Lippe. 1824-58, including
the 1, 2, 3 and 4 Pfg, last coinage. Unc., red. Others fair
to fine.   32

285   Schemnitz. 1702 C S linked. Schlesien. 1797 ½ Kreutzer.
Schleusingen. Heller, 1705-17 (4). Schmalkalden. Heller, 1744, '45. Schömberg. A cask, above D ✠ F below, 1771
vine around border. ℞ Plain. A fine and large Token, size
35. Schönau. 4 Heller. Fair to good.   10

286   Schwarzburg-Rudolstadt. 1, 2, 3, 4 Pfenning, 1751-1825 (14).
— Sondershausen, ⅛, ¼, 1 Krzr, 1, 3 Pfg (13). Seelfeld.
1731 Brewery Token. Silesia. ½ Krzr, 1788-1806, F W
cwnd, 1796 ½ Gros., 1797 Solidus, ½, 1 and 3 Gros. Most
good to fine.   38

287   Soest. 1620 2 Schil. (sm. hole), 3 Pfg, 1714-44 (10). Speyer,
Stolberg (3), Stralsund (16)07, Scherf, 1622 6 Pfg. Styria.
Raitpfennig, bust of Ferd. Tecklenburg-Rheda. 1760-61
3, 6 Pfg (3). Tyrol. 1809 Kreutzer. Transylvania. 1764
Greschl. Fair to fine.   22

288   Torgau. (15)49 BRAW . ZCIEC(he .) STAT TORGAW . Arms,
CS. above 4/9 ℞ Incuse of obv. Fine, rare. 31.   1

289 Another. BRAV | ZEICHE . | DER . STAT . | TORGAW 1.5.8.9
℞ Arms. Very good, rare ; lozenge form 41 x 39.   1

290 Treves. ¼, ½ Krzr, 2 Pfennigs, 1773–89. Teutonic Order.
1622 2 Pfennigs. Ulm. Heller, n.d. and blank *revs.* (6
slightly varying), 4 do. sim., 1772, '73 Krzrs. Mostly very
good.   13

291 Vienna. Poorhouse Tokens for 1, 4 and 12 Pfg, 1728–73 Hd
of Christ *l.* Fine. 18 to 26.   4

292 Waldeck. 1622 to 1867 1 Pfg (18), 3 do, (9), 4 do. (1), 6 do.
(1). Mostly very good.   29

293 Warburg. 1622 4 Pfg. Warendorf. 1613 6 Pfg, Portcullis,
1676 Heller, sim., 1690 Pfg, St. Laurentius stdg. Weisen-
burg. 1622 Krzr. Wolgast. 1592 Witten. Good, all
rare.   6

294 Weid, and Weid-Runkel. 1749–58 ¼ Stubers (7). Westphalia.
(16)83 Tower and archway, V above, arms below, 1808–12
1 Pfg and 1, 2, 3, 5 Ctms. Wismar. 3 Pfg, 1824–50 (9).
Good to fine.   28

295 Westphalia. Jerome Napoleon, 1808 Pattern 1, 2, 3 and 5 Ctms,
by *Toilier.* HN linked. ℞ Legend incuse on raised border.
Same as adopted design. *m.m.* J. Symbol, a horse's head.
Unc., partly bright, rare.   4

296 Wimpen. 1539, '49, '58, '70 and 2 without date, 3 Krzr and
possibly other values. Trunk of tree surmounted by W sep.
date. All with blank *revs.* Good, rare. 25 to 28 (6).
Ysenburg. A snipe *l.* Tokens of the hunt (2 var.). Good.
18.   8

297 Wurtemburg. 1621 Bracteate, 1842–71 ¼ Krzr (5), 1842–63 ½
do. (12). Wurzburg. ¼, ½, 1 Krzr, ½, 3 Pfg, 1751–1811
(17). Good to very fine.   35

DUPLICATES AND DIE-VARIETIES.

298 Unassorted duplicates and die varieties of the preceding
German coins. Condition fair to fine. Aachen (2), An-
halt (5, including a duplicate of Tax Token same as
in lot 192), Augsburg (2), Austria (25), Baden (23),
Bavaria (17), Brandenburg (11), Bremen (5), Brunswick-
Luneburg (28).   118

299 Unassorted duplicates and die-varieties of the preceding German coins. Burgau (3), Camenz, Chur-Pfalz (2), Constance, Corvey (2), Dantzic (2), Eimbeck (4), Frankfort (11), Fulda, Galicia (3), Goslar (4), Gottingen, Hamm (5), Hervord, Hesse (32), Hildesheim, Hungary (5), Lend, Limb. and Breit, Lippe (6), Lowenstein-Wert. (4), Mecklenburg (11), etc. 105

300 — Lowenstein-Werth. (4), Mentz (7), Munster (25), Nassau (8), Nassau-Orange (3), Nuremburg (a duplicate of lot 263 and equally as good), Oldenburg (5), Osnabruck, Paderborn (4), Pomerania, Posen, Prussia (29), Reuss (10), Rostock (14). 113

301 — Salzburg (4), Saxony (51), Schaumberg-Hesse (5), —Lippe (7), Schw.-Rudolstadt (4), — Sondershausen (4), Soest (2), Torgaw (a duplicate of lot 289, in good condition), Waldeck (21), Weid (2), Westphalia (4), Wismar, Wurtemberg (4), Wurzburg (8). 118

301a Various uncirculated duplicates, all bright red. 2 of last century, but mostly late, 13 differing. 32

302 Unattributed and unknown to me, 16th to 19th century. Square, oblong and circular; some uniface. Initials, mongrams, arms and various devices. A remarkable and interesting collection; at least one quarter are coins, the remainder are tokens and probably not all German. Mostly good, 3 holed. 64

303 — Others, in lead, 1564, 1725 and without date. Good. 16 to 38 (2 of the largest size). 9

304 Mintmasters' Jetons, 1568–1778, chiefly of Zellerfeld, a variety of designs and dates. Many good to fine. 42

305 Jetons, by Egidius and Hans Krauwinkel, Conrad, Hans and Wolf Laufer, Schlemm and others; chiefly of Nuremberg. Some are fine work and early, 1538, '75, '78, '80 and later, many undated, a great number of designs with die-varieties of a few. Good to fine, 1 holed. 83

306 — Others, in brass, similar to preceding, very few are dated; many late, some refer to the wars of 1812–15. Busts of Luther, Blucher, etc. Mostly good to fine. 43

307 Rechenpfennigs or Counters, by the Krauwinkels, Laufers, etc., 1568, '80, 1601, '09 and later, but mostly undated. Fair to fine, 3 holed. Copper and brass. 42

308 Rechenpfennigs or Counters. Man at table counting. ℞ The alphabet, numerous varieties, all early and probably Nuremburg make. Fair to fine, 6 holed.   24

309 Abbey Pieces. Fleurs-de-lis in shld, Lion of St. Mark, Crown, Cross and other types, with varying legends, but chiefly AVE MARIA and mystical arrangements of letters. A great variety, though no attempt has been made to assort them for duplicates. This with the 2 following lots are about equal as to size and condition ; about all grades of the latter will be found, but the average is good.   58

310 Another, similar.   79

311 Another, similar.   85

312 Unassorted duplicates of Jetons, Mintmasters' Tokens and Rechenpfennigs. Good, fine.   60

313 The poor and holed of German Coins, Jetons, etc., including a very fair duplicate of Munster (lot 256), Bela of Hungary, and many others of interest. Mostly early.   111

314 Cards, Checks, Brewery Tokens, Medalets, etc. Including Berlin Numismatic Soc., 1876. Mostly late. Copper and brass. Good to fine.   30

315 Switzerland. Aargau, Appenzell, Basle, Geneva, Lucerne, Ticino, Zug, Zurich and other Cantons. Angester, Centimes, Rappen, etc., 1795–1876. A few issued as base, now appearing same as copper. Good to fine.   51

316 — Neuchatel. Alex., 1814 Head r. by *Droz*. ℞ 2 | FRANCS within wreath. Inscribed edge (in relief). *Pattern*. About perfect, medium olive color.   1

ITALY, SICILY, SARDINIA.

317 Ancona. Rep., 1200–1300 (6) Pius V, Sixtus V, Quattrini and Sesini. Poor to v. good. Pius VI, 1796 1 and 2½ Baiocchi. Good. Aquila, Inn. VII, Chas. VII, etc., Cavallo (5). Fair to good.   15

318 Ascoli. Alex. VI, Quat. Bologna. Anonymous Papal, prior to 1431. Clem. VIII, with bust, also Lion with flag. 1609– 1755 (13) Pius VI, Arms, 1778–84 (3), all Quat. Lion without flag, Half Bai., 1624–1753 (9). Fair to good.   29

319 Differing dates of the last three described and not contained therein, 1610–1784. Mostly good.   25

320 1781, '84 ½ Bai., 1780, '84 1 do. Arms in shield. 1795, '96
     Quat., 1796 ½ and 2 (2 var.) Bai. Dancing lion. Most fine.
     27–37.   9

321 1781, '84 (2 var.) ½ Bai., 1780, '81 1 do., 1796 Quat. and 2
     Bai., marked varieties of the preceding, also Pattern 20 Ctmi,
     1860, with silver centre. Good to fine.   8

322 Bozzolo, 1609–71, Brindisi, 1198–1250 Quat., Cagliari, Chas.
     II of Spain, 1669 1 Cagliari, 1668, '69, '85 3 do. with bust
     (thick), Chas. VI, 1713 3 do., and another late issue, un-
     dated. Good to fine.   8

323 Camerino, Casale (1630, 10 Florins, holed, poor, rare), Casti-
     glione (4), Castro (2), Cattaro, Chieti, Correggio (3), Fano
     (5), 14th to 16th century, Quat., Sesini, etc. Fair to good.   18

324 Carrara. Early Tesserae, various designs, but chiefly a winged
     figure sep. F—F (prob. for Francisco Foscari, a Venetian
     moneyer about 1480). ℞ A four-wheeled chariot? Unas-
     sorted, probably but few if any duplicates. Good to fine.
     19 to 31.   54

325 Casale. 1630 20 Florins. INSTAR HORVM, etc., 3 fleurs-de-lis
     in cwnd shld sep. F — XX Ex. CASALE ℞ Justice stdg be-
     fore female leaning against column. Duby, Plate II, No.
     14. Good, very rare. 40.   1

326 Civita Vecchia. 1796 2½ Bai., '97 do. (2 var.) Bust of St.
     Peter, 1797 5 Bai., Bust of the Blessed Virgin (3 var.). Fair
     to v. good. Dalmatia and Albania. 1 Gazetta (3 var.), 2
     do. (2 var.). Etruria. 1804, '05 2 Soldi. Good to unc.   13

327 — Die-varieties of last. 2½ Bai., 1796 (2), 5 do., 1797 (2).
     Dalm. and Alb. 1 Gaz. (2), 2 do. (2). Fair to good.   8

328 Fermo. Rep., 1220–1331 Sesino. Size 16. Pius VI, 1796,
     '97 2½ Bai., 1797 5 do. Under Roman Rep., 1798 ½ Bai.
     (2 types), 1 do. (3 types), 2 do. (3 types). Mostly good to
     fine, none common, some rare. 25 to 36.   12

329 Ferrara. Alfonzo I, Quat. and Papal issues from Clem. VIII,
     1598–1605 to Benedict XIV, 1740–58, including 10 reigns.
     Quat. ½ and 1 Baiocco. An extensive and interesting col-
     lection. Many large. Mostly good.   58

330 Fuligno. Pius VI, Quat. (holed), ½, 1, 2 Bai. with Pontifical
     year, 1794 1 Bai., '95 2 do., '96, '97 2½ do. Good to fine,
     scarce coins. 21 to 37.   8

331 Florence. Savings Ass'n Token for 1 Lira (late). Genoa. 1699–1814 4 Denari, 2, 4, 10 Soldi. Some issued as base coins, also Municipal Tax Token, for 40 Litri of Common Wine. Size 37. Good. 22

332 Goritz. $\frac{1}{2}$, 1, 2, 3 Soldi (the last, size 35), 1733–36, an uncommon set. Other Soldi $\frac{1}{2}$ (2), 1 (10), 2 (1), 1741–1800. Guastalla. Ferd. II, 1621 and Ferd. III, n.d., Sesini. Gd to unc., 2 bright red. 19

333 Gubbio. Inn. XII (2), Clem. XI (3), Inn. XIII, Benedict XIII (2), all Quat. 1723, '25 $\frac{1}{2}$ Bai., 1726–29 1 Bai. (5), Clem. XII, 1738, '39 and n. d., Quat. (6), 1739 $\frac{1}{2}$ Bai, 1730–38 1 Bai (6). Good to fine, many large. 27

334 — Benedict XIV, 1740 and n.d. Quat. (5), 1744–57 $\frac{1}{2}$ Bai. (9), 1742–55 1 do. (12), Clem. XIII, 1759 Quat., $\frac{1}{2}$ Bai and 1 do. (3), Pius VI, years 15 to 20, $\frac{1}{2}$ Bai. (2), 1 do. (3), and 2 do., 1796 $2\frac{1}{2}$ do., bust of St. Peter, 1797 5 do., bust of the B. V., also $\frac{1}{2}$ do. (2), with ins. only. Fair to fine, mostly v. good. 41

335 Italy. Rep., 1804 REPUBBLICA ITALIANA wheat heads. 1, 2 Denari. Scales. $\frac{1}{100}$ Lira, $\frac{1}{2}$, 1 Soldo. Unc., all red or partly so, rare. 17 to 27. 5

336 — Napoleon I, Centesimo, 1808–13 (14), 3 do., 1807–13 (11), 5 do., 1807–13 (13). Mints B(ologna), M(ilan) and V(enice). Mostly good to unc., a few are bright red. 38

337 — Vic. Em. II, 1 (4), 2 (5), 5 (5) and 10 (10) Centimes, 1861–67. Mints of Milan, Naples, Turin, etc. Mostly unc., some bright red. 24

338 Lombardy-Venice. 1 Ctmo (12) 1822, 3 do. (12) 1822–52, 5 do. (10) 1822–50, 10 do. 1849. Under Austria. 1852 1, 3, 5 (2 each), 10 and 15 Ctmi. 2d coinage, 1862 $\frac{5}{10}$ (2), 1 (3) Ctmo. Various mints, mostly Milan and Venice. Many fine, 13 unc. 48

339 Lucca. Rep., 1369–1805. The early and undated (6). Others 1691–1790. Felix and Eliza, 1806 (their busts conjoined in profile) and Chas. Louis to 1841. Quat., Soldi, Centesimi, etc. Good to fine, late ones very choice and desirable. 24

340 Macerata. 15th century. Greg. XIII. Italian Rep., $\frac{1}{2}$ Bai. (1798–99) rare. Massa, 1792 (2). Mirandola, 1637–91. Modena. Fran. I, 1629–58 to Hercules II, 1783 Quat., Sesini, Bolognini, Soldi, etc. Mostly very good. 18

341 Mantua. Francis II, 1484–1519 to siege of the city 1799, at
   least 12 reigns. Many with portraits, some with Virgilius
   Maro, others have arms, sun in flames, etc. Quat., Sesini,
   Soldi, etc. Fair to fine.   73

342 Milan. G. M. Sforza, 1466–76 to Maria Theresa, 1779. Including Chas. V, Phil. II, III, IV and Chas. II (all Spanish
   kings). Trelina, Quat., Sesini, Soldi, etc., also a late Theatre
   Token, size 37. Mostly good, 3 unc., red.   33

343 Monaco. Anton, 1720 8 Den. (piece from edge), Honore V,
   1837, '38 5 Ctms and Dcmo, each in Æ and brass, also Patterns for same, 1838 (proofs). Montalto. 1797 2½, 5 Bai.
   (only fair, but rare). Montanaro. 1529–42, Mtd horseman.
   Montferrat. Wm. II, 1494–1518 (2, one with bust. ℞ Stag.
   Very good. Size 31), Geo., 1530–33. Musso. Jno. Jas.,
   1528–32. ℞ A river-god. Good to fine.   14

344 Naples and Sicily. Roger, 1085–1111 to Fred. III, 1496–1500,
   including 13 reigns, a few with portraits, others with face
   of lion, arms, etc. Arabic inscriptions, some Arabic and
   Latin. A few on concave planchets. Fair to good. 12
   to 27.   31

345 — A sim. asst. (die-varieties). Roger, 1085–1111 to Chas.
   and Joanna, 1516–20, 13 reigns. Fair to good.   27

346 — Chas. V (1st of Spain), 1520–56 1, 2, 3 Cavalli, last 2 with
   portrait, also Jeton, 1553 (9), Phil. II, 1556–98 1, 2, 4 Cavalli (10), the latter dated. Fair to good.   19

347 — A very sim. asst. from varying dies, those dated differ from
   preceding. Fair to good.   17

348 — Phil. III, 1598–1621 Grano, 3, 4 Cavalli and Cinquina, the
   last 3 dated (18). Insurrection, Henry of Lorraine, 1648 1,
   2, 3 Tornesi. Fair to good.   21

349 — Phil. IV, 1621–65, various Cavalli, Tornesi and Grani, all
   with bust. *Revs.* Fleece, castle, cross, etc. (14). Chas. II,
   1665–1700, sim. values, mostly with dates (14). Fair to gd.
   16 to 30.   28

350 — Die varieties of Phil. III (6), Henry of Lorraine (3), Phil.
   IV (11), Chas. II (6), representing most of the values in the
   2 preceding lots. Fair to good.   26

351 — Phil. V (3), Vic. Amadeus (12), Chas. III (VI) 3, Chas. of
   Bourbon (12), Tornesi, Cavalli, etc. Fair to good. 16 to 30. 30

352	Naples and Sicily. Ferd. IV, 3, 4, 6, 9, 12 Cavalli, 1, 2, 5, 10 Grani, 1776–1804, various types. Many good to fine, some uncommon.	49
353	— Others. 4, 5, 6, 8, 10 Tornesi, 1797–1800, 1, 2, 5, 10 Grani, 1814–15, Grapes, Pegasus, setd female and cornucopias, also 5 Tornesi, 1817. Mostly good, a few fine.	18
354	— 1814–15, set of 1, 2, 5 and 10 Grani. Head *r.*, cwnd. ℞ Grapes, Pegasus, etc., as last described. Sharp, unc., all partly bright.	4
355	— 1816 5, 8 Tornesi, 1817 1, 4, 8 do., 1819 5, 10 do. Unc., red. Gems.	7
356	— Murat. 1810 2 Grana (2), 3 do. (5) die-varieties, 1813 Pattern 2 Lire. Good, all uncommon. Fran. II, 1859 2, 10 Tornesi. V. fine, partly bright.	10
357	— Others of Murat. 1810 2 and 3 Grana. Unc., red. 1813 10 Centesimi with a very dif. hd. Fine, all rare. 28, 34, 36.	3
358	— Fran. I, 1, 2, 5 and 10 Tornesi, 1825–27. Unc., red. 19 to 38.	4
359	— Ferd. II, ½ Tornese, 1833, '35, '38, '49, '53, 1 do., 1840, '54, 1½ do., 1836, '39, '40, 2 do., 1839, '43, '52, '56, '58, 3 do., 1833, '39, '51. Unc., all red or partly so.	18
360	— Others. 1832–51, dates differing from those in preceding lot, ½ Tornese (2), 1 do. (3), 1½ do. (2), 2 do. (3), 3 do. (2), 5 do. (5), 10 do. (9). Good to fine.	26
361	— Another lot, 1831–59. Similarly asst., quite the equal and not duplicating dates in either of the preceding.	27
362	Novellara. Alf. II, Sesino, Orbetello, 1, 2, 4 Quat., 1782–98 (11). Padua. 13th century. Palma Nuova. Siege of 1814, under Nap. I, 50 Centimes. Rare. Good to fine.	14

The series of Papal coins following usually have the arms of the reigning Pope, a few have their portraits, others bear the bust of St. Paul or St. Peter. Those which have ROMANO or its abbreviation (excepting the mint-mark R.) are classified under Rome.

363	Papal. Paul II, 1464–71 to Clement VIII, 1592–1605 (including 9 reigns), all Quattrini. Fair to good, some fine.	22
364	— Clem. VIII, 1592–1605 to Alex. VII, 1655–67. Six consecutive Popes. Quat. and ½ Bai. Mostly good.	19
365	— Clem. IX, 1667–79 to Alex. VIII, 1689–91 (4 reigns, complete chronology). Quat. and ½ Bai. Good, 1 holed.	25

366 Papal. Inn. XII, 1691–1700 Quat. (12), ½ Bai. (4). Clem. XI, 1700–21 Quat. (10), ½ Bai. (3). Good, some are fine. 29

367 — Inn. XIII, 1721–24 (7),Benedict XIII (5), Clem. XII (8), Benedict XIV (15), Clem. XIII, 1758–69 (3). Mostly Quattrini. Good, some fine. 38

368 — Pius VI, 1, 2, 5 Bai., all undated, 1797 5 do. (unc.), also 1799, 2 var. of same. The 5 Bai. has bust of Virgin, Sancta Dei Genetrix. Good to fine, a lot of more than ordinary interest, some are rare. 6

369 — 1801–22 Last coinage of Pius VI, Quat. (7), ½ Bai. (7), 1 do. (5). Gregory XVI, Quat. (8), ½ Bai. (16), 1 do. (17), differing years and mints, 1831–45. Good to unc., many bright red. 60

369a — Greg. XVI, ½ Bai., 1844, CS. CERVARO, 1 do., 1836, CS. PONTE MOLLE. Both holed near edge. 2

370 — Pius IX, 1848 2 Bai. (3), 3 do. (3), each on a thick and thin planchet in Æ, and thick in brass. Also Scudo in Æ and brass. Patterns in proof, struck at the Gaëte mint. Rare. 8

371 — Pius IX, 1850 ½, 1, 2 Bai., 1851 ½, 1, 5 Bai. Proofs from Rome mint. 6

372 — Quat. (1), ½ Bai. (7), 1 do. (8), 2 do. (7), 5 do. (8), 1846–54. All Rome mint. Good to unc., one half partly bright to full red. 37

373 — Quat. (1), ½ Bai. (6), 1 do. (7), 2 do. (5), 5 do. (4), 1846–54. All Bologna mint. Mostly v. good, 2 unc. Last Papal coinage. Bust of Pius IX, 1 Centesimo (2), 2½ do. (2), 5 do. (3), 10 do. (2), 20 do. (6). Fine to unc. 38

374 Parma. Alex. Farnese, 1587–92 to Ferd. of Bourbon, 1795 Quat., Sesini and Soldi. Good to fine. Also Maria Louise, 1830 1, 3, 5 Ctmi. Unc. 28

375 Passerano. 1581–98 Quat. Percola. 1798 1 Bai. Perugia. 1250–1506 (5), 1795 2 Bai., arms, 1796, '97 2½ do., bust of St. Peter, 1797 ½ do., arms, also 5 do. with bust of the Virgin. Mostly good, some fine, several rare. 13

376 Pesaro. John Sforza, 1489–1510 (7). Piacenza, with bust of St. Anton. Piedmont. Piombino, 1693, etc. (3). Pisa. 1313–1494 Quat., Soldi, etc. Fair to good. 13

377 Ravenna. Benedict XIV, Quat. (11), ½ Bai. (6). Ragusa, 12th to 15th cent. Follaro (4), 1731–93 Soldi (6), Mezzanino (2). Reggio. Hercules I, 1471–1505, Alfonzo I and Her. II (6), Quat. Fair to good. 40

378 Rome. Papal issues with Rom., Roma, Romano or Romani. Pope Urban VIII, Clement XII, 1738 to Clement XIII, 1759 Quattrini (7), ½ Baioccho (9), 1 do. (9). Many good to fine. 26

379 — Another similar selection within same period, duplicating none of the preceding. Good to fine. 23

380 — Pius VI, year of reign and 1795–97 to Greg. XVI, 1834 Quat., ½, 1, 2 and 2½ Bai., includes some of the largest Papal issues. Mostly good to fine, a few unc. 26

381 — A very similar assortment in same reigns, duplicating none of the preceding. Same condition, more of the uncirculated. 22

382 Roman Republic. 1798–99 REPVBBLICA ROMANA Two fasces. ℞ VN | BAIOCCO in frame. Another, eagle on fasces, within wrth. ℞ DVE | BA | IOCCHI within triangle of fasces. Border of dots. V. fine, rare. 29½, 34. 2

383 — 2 Baiocchi. Flags, fasces and Lib. pole crossed. ℞ Value in triangle, branches at sides. 35. Another, Rep — Rom | an — 7 R (in script) separated by fasces. ℞ 2 | Baiocchi (also script) coarsely executed. From Anthon sale, 1188. Good. 35. Both rare. 2

384 — Two Baiocchi. Fasces. ℞ Value within wreath. Various, by the famous die-cutters, Hamerani, Mercandetti and Perpenti, with some unsigned, 2 have m.m. A(ncona) in field. Differing letters, spelling, and binding of fasces. Good to fine. 10

385 — ½ Bai. of same design, 2 from dif. dies, also a duplicate of the last 2 Bai. in lot 382, but on planchet size 32. 1849 1 Bai., cast at Ancona, also ½, 1 and 3 (2 mints) do., Eagle within wreath. Good to unc., none common, some rare. 8

386 Ronciglione. 1799 3 Bai., FIDELITA RELIGIONE Bust of Virgin. ℞ The city in flames. Others, sim., FIDELITA E RELIGIONE ℞ Value and date in 4 lines, one with reversed figures in date. Fair to good, all rare. 3

387 Sabionetta. Vespanio, 1539–91, Caraffa and Isabel, 1591–
1638. St. Martin. S. Gonzaga, 1639–71. Sienna, 1404–
55 (2). Spalato, 1491–1500 (2). Urbino. Guido Ubaldo
I, 1500–08 to F. Maria II, 1574–1622 (21). Quat., Bagattini
and Sesini, also Scudo in Æ of F. Maria II, 1621, holed near
edge, otherwise fine. Mostly good. 29

388 San Marino. 1864, '69 5 Ctmi, 1875 10 do. San Severino.
1769 (1796) 2½ Bai. Others, ½, 2½ and 5 Bai., 1796, '97 and
n.d., all in time of Pius VI. Mostly v. good, some fine and
scarce. 17

389 Sardinia, the kingdom. Vic. Am. II, Chas. Em. IV and Chas.
Felix, 1688–1826 2 Denari, ½, 1, 5 and 7½ Soldi, 1, 2 and 3
Ctmi. Two each of last, varieties in letters and symbols be-
low wreath on obv. Good to unc., red. 33

390 — The Island. Chas. VI, 1712 to Chas. Albert, 1842 1, 3
Cagliari, 2 Denari, Soldi and Ctmi. Mostly very good. 30

391 Savoy. Chas. Em., 1580–1630 (7), Tivoli, 1795 5 Bai. Tuscany. Ferd. II, 1620–70 to Vic. Em., 1859 (set, unc.) Quat.,
Soldi and Ctmi. Good to fine. 62

392 Venice. Fran. Foscari, 1423–57 to Louis Manin, 1789–97 Bag-
attino, Quat., Sesino, ½ and 1 Soldi (6 and 12 Deniers).
Representing 34 different Doges. Mostly v. good. 46

392a Anonymous. Quat. Lion in frame, many varieties of letters.
Bizzone, Madonna, and half length figure of St. Paul, with
other oddities (2 square). Prov. Govt., 1849. 1, 3, 5 Ctmi
and Jeton undated. Good to fine. 31

393 Vicenza. Phil. III, 1611 Quat. Viterbo. Sixtus IV, 1471–84
Quat., Pius VI, 1796 2½ Bai., '97 5 do. Good to fine. 4

SLAVIC STATES.

394 Poland. Jno. Casimir, 1650 Solidus, J.C.R. linked and cwnd.
℞ Eagle. Another, sim. ℞ Ins. and date. Cracow. 1835
Pattern 3 Groze, and a Token by Count Zamoski. Good to
fine, all rare. 4

395 — Others of Poland. John Casimir (a few for Lithuania)
1661 to Nich. I, 1840, differing dates and types of Solidus,
Schillings and Groze. Mostly v. good. 69

396 Finland. Alex. II and III, 1865–83 1 Penni (14), 5 do. (7),
10 do. (4). Good to unc. 25

⟨ 397   Moldavia and Wallachia. Cath. II, 1771 3 Denga. E II
       cwnd. ℞ Dbl-hd eagle (2 var., small and large letters).
       Rare. Others, 2 shields cwnd, 3 Denga 1772, 3 Kopecks
       1772, '73, 74. V. fair to v. good.   6

398   — 1772 3 Denga and 3 Kopecks, type as last described. Fine.   2

399   Crimea. Tschal, 5th year = 1781–82 Toghra. ℞ Inscription
       bet. year and date. Borders plain. Fon., 6727. Fine, rare.
       51.   1

400   — Another, sim. 6th year, Toghra bet. flowers. Fine, rare.
       51.   1

401   — A dif. design, with ins. in 4 lines, without Toghra. Utsch-
       Beschlik, Besch-Beschlik, and Kyrmis, 4th, 5th and 3d years
       = 1783–79. Fine. Smallest holed. Rare set. 20, 28, 45.   3

402   — 1239 = 1823–24, a large flat ring 13 *mlm.* stamped with
       Toghra, date and value (?) Good, rare. 59.   1

403   Circassia. Oblongs (4), one with sword. Georgia. Thamar,
       1184–1212, Phu and Falus (Fon., 4236, 4241), and others of
       Enekle II, 1762–98 1 and 2 Bisti, with dates 1782 to 1796.
       Eagle displayed. Thick coins, poor to good, all rare. 22
       to 30.   12

404   Georgia. Others with fish (4), peacock and bird (7), goat,
       etc. (7). Poor and fair, they rarely appear otherwise.   18

405   — Others, lion *r.* and *l.*, and some with sun. Poor and
       fair.   14

406   Tiflis. Alex. I, 1801–25 5 (?), 10 and 20 Phuli. Under a crown,
       Tiflis in Georgian, branches crossed below. Fine, rare. 20,
       25, 32.   3

407   — Others of varying dates, 10 Phuli (4), 20 do. (2). Good to
       fine.   6

408   Moscow, Twer and early Russian, all prior to 1700. Various
       designs, mostly oblong, and small. Poor to gd, the medium
       quality prevails.   31

409   Another quite as varying as the preceding, both unassorted,
       probably a few are in duplicate, condition as last.   32

410   Roumania. 1867 1, 2, 5, 10 Bani. Unc., red. Servia. Michl
       III, 1868 1, 5, 10 Para. Fine to unc. Bulgaria. 1879
       Jeton, 1880, '87 Essais for 10 Ctms, 1881 5, 10 Stotinki,
       1888 2½, 5, 10, 20 do., the last set in *nickel.* Mostly in mint
       state.   16

_? 411   Turkey.   Abdul-Medjid, 1839–61 1 (2), 5 (4), 10 (3), 40 (6)
            Paras.   Abdul-Aziz, 1861–76 5, 10, 20 (2 each) and 40 (unc.)
            do.   All dif. dates.   Mostly fine.   24

    412   Greece.   Capo D'Istria, 1828 1, 5, 10 Lepta, 1830 1, 5, 10 (2
            var.) do., 1831, 1, 10, 20 do.   All with phoenix.   Gd to fine.   10

    413   — Otho, 1833–62 1 (4), 2 (8), 5 (10), 10 (11) Lepta.   George
            I, 1863— 1, 2, 5 (2), 10 (2) do.   Good to unc., 5 of latter.   39

ISLANDS OF THE MEDITERRANEAN SEA.

    414   Armata and Morea.   1, 2 Soldini.   Candia.   2 (2), 2½ do. and
            60 Tornesi (IIII).   Isole and Armata.   1, 2 Soldini.   Corfu,
            Ceph. and Zante.   1, 2 do.   All under Venetian rule.   Good
            to fine, some rare.   11

    415   Corsica.   Theo., 1736 5 Soldi.   T. R. cwnd.   Obv. good, rev.
            barely fair; very rare.   21.   1

    416   — Pascal Paoli, 1768 1 Soldo, hat on pole, 1764–67 4 do. (6),
            small bust in cwnd shld.   Cyprus.   Jas. II, 1464–73 Cavallo,
            1570 Bisante.   Victoria, 1879 ¼, ½ Cent, 1881 ¼ do.   Good
            to fine.   12

    417   Ionian Isles.   Under Russian Protection.   1801 10 Gazetti.
            Lion of St. Mark.   Legend, etc. in Greek.   Gd, v. rare.   36.   1

    418   — English Protection.   1819 2½, 5, 10 Oboli, 1820 2½ do.,
            1834–62 1 Obolus (5).   Good.   9

    419   Malta.   John de la Valette, 1557–68 to Emmanuel de Rohan,
            1775–97, representing 15 Grand Masters.   Piccioli, Grani
            and Tari, various denominations of each, a few are CS.   Fair
            to fine, but mostly good.   The most extensive collection of-
            fered in many years, if indeed it has ever been equalled in
            the United States.   58

    420   Varieties and duplicates of the preceding, representing 8 Grand
            Masters, 1557–1797.   A few poor, but mostly v. fair to good.   49

AFRICA.

    421   Alexandria.   1861 Merchant's Token (twice holed).   Algiers.
            (1827–28) Aspers (2), Paras (2).   Angola (Portuguese Af-
            rica).   5 Reis, 1770, ¼ Macuta, 1770, ½ do., 1814, '53, '58,
            2 do. with entire edge battered, nevertheless a rare coin.   Gd
            to fine.   Congo.   1887, '88, '89 1, 2, 5, 10 Ctms (only 1888
            complete).   Unc.   19

422 Angola. Jos. I, 1763 ½ Macuta. Unc., partly red, v. choice. Maria and Peter, 1785 1 do. Very good. Large and rare coins and usually counterstamped, these are not. 37, 42. — 2

423 Egypt. Achmed I, 1603–17 and later, Abdul Hamid I, Mahmud II, etc., to present coinage, 4, 5, 10, 20, 40 Para, including a Pattern 20 Para (1863), Fon. 5220, ¼, ½, 1, 2, 5 Ochr'-el-Guerche, chiefly of this century. Good to unc. — 36

424 French West Africa (French Congo). 1883 1, 5, 10 Ctms. Obvs. and revs. alike. Unc., rare ; brass. 17, 19, 20. — 3

425 Gold Coast. Geo. III, 1796 1 Takoe. G. R. crowned. ℞ Arms. A bronzed proof, rare. 17. — 1

426 Griquatown. GRIQUA — TOWN ¼. ℞ A bird. Very fine, very rare. 20. — 1

427 Liberia. 1833 Cent, 1847 1, 2 do., 1862 1 do. German E. Africa. 1890 Pice and a poor Griquatown ¼. Good to unc. — 6

428 Liberia. 1862 1, 2 Cents, 1866 Pattern 1, 2 do. All proofs. — 4

429 Morocco. 1223–88 = 1808–72 Var. of 1, 2 and 3 Falus, all with star. Fair to good. — 17

430 Mozambique. 1840 20, 40, 80 Reis, 1853 1 and 2 do. Complete set, in fine preservation, very rare, especially the 80 R. 14½ to 36. — 5

431 Oran. Phil., 1618 2 Rls and n.d. 4 and 8 do. Cwnd arms. ℞ o | RA | N. Chas. II, 169(1) and n.d. 4 and 8 Rls. ℞ I. H. S. Very fair to about good, planchets imperfect, have never seen them otherwise. I do not know of another set in this country. Very rare. — 5

432 Sierra Leone. 1791 1 Cent, 1 Penny, 10 Cents (bronzed proofs), and 1 Dol., very fine ; the last 2 are from dies for siver coins. — 4

433 Suez Canal. 1865 50 Ctms and 1 Franc. Ship sailing r. Brass, unc. Zanzibar. 1299, 1304 Cents of dif. type, 1881, '87. V. fine. — 4

434 Tripoli. II–Λ–Λ (= 1774/5) on sides of triangle, also 1223 = 1808/9 and n.d., all Paras. Tunis. Mostafa III, 1751/74 to Abdul-Aziz, 1861/76 Aspers, Berben, Caroubs, representing 7 coinages. Good to fine. 11 to 34. — 26

435 **Islands adjacent.** Azores. 1750–1880 5, 10, 20 Reis (13). Bourbon. 1779 3 Sols. Poor. Madeira. 1842 10, 20 Reis, 1852 10 do. Mauritius. 1877 1, 2, 5 Cents. St. Helena (2). Mostly very good.   22

436 Mauritius. Victoria, 1888 1, 2 and 5 Cents, in red mint state.   3

437 St. Thomas and Principe. 1819 80 Reis (brilliant), 1825 Same value, good, edge dent. ATA in *mon.* and 1853 each CS. in circle 12 *mlm.* above ST THOMAS stamped on English Penny (1797). Holed.   3

438 Terceira. Maria II, 1829 80 Reis. Cast from bells during the Queen's flight to the island. Good, rare.   1

439 Cape of Good Hope, Griquatown (2), Liberia (12), Madagascar, Orange Free State (3), So. African Rep. (2). All red and brilliant.   21

The next preceding are unsolicited and unauthentic patterns, and as clearly barefaced impositions ; the result of a European *business* venture to manufacture coins for small or obscure countries for the sole purpose of selling them to collectors ; it began about 1878 and reached its climax in 1892.

440 Mahometan Dynasty, 622–1031, probably includes some of the later period to 1492. A variety of types, chiefly in arrangement of legends and inscriptions, all of which are in Arabic, some have inscription within circle, others in square frame, also in 8-ptd star. Unassorted, poor to good.   70

441 Another lot selected from the whole, and intended to be the equal of the preceding.   75

442 Another, similar.   75

443 Coins of the Caliphs, 632–1171 and possibly later. Deities, heads, busts and mtd horsemen. Inscriptions and legends in Arabic. Poor to good. 18 to 30.   29

ASIA.

444 Siberia. (Unsurpassed.) Cath. II, 1764 ¼, ½, 1, 2, 5 and 10 Kopecks. Two sables support cwnd shld, within which value and date. ℞ Large E. II cwnd, the smallest is without sables. Unc., red. Sizes 18 to 47.   6

444a — 1767 Set, lacking 1 and 10 Kop. Uncirculated, red.   4

445 — 1768 Set complete. Uncirculated, red.   6

446 — 1769 Set as last. Uncirculated, red.   6

447 — 1770 Set as last. Uncirculated, red.   6

448	Siberia. 1771 Set as last. Uncirculated, red.	6
449	— 1772 Set as last. Uncirculated, red.	6
450	— 1773 Set as last. Uncirculated, red.	6
451	— 1774 Set as last. Uncirculated, red.	6
452	— 1775 Set as last. Uncirculated, red.	6
453	— 1776 Set as last. Uncirculated, red.	6
454	— 1777 Set, lacking the 5 Kop. Uncirculated, red.	5
455	— 1778 Set, lacking ¼ and ½ Kop. Uncirculated, red.	4
456	— 1779 Set complete. Uncirculated, red.	6
457	— 1780 Set complete. Uncirculated, red.	6
458	— Others, good to fine. 1767 1, 2, 5 and 10 Kop.	4
459	— 1775 1, 2, 5 and 10 Kopecks.	4
460	— 1768 Set complete.	6
461	— 1769 Set complete.	6
462	— 1770 ¼, ½, 2, 5 and 10 Kopecks.	5
463	— 1771 ½, 1, 2, 5 and 10 Kopecks.	5
464	— 1772 1, 2, 5 and 10 Kopecks.	4
465	— 1773 ¼, ½, 2, 5 and 10 Kopecks.	5
466	— 1774 ½, 1, 2, 5 and 10 Kopecks.	5
467	— 1776 1, 2, 5 and 10 Kopecks.	4
468	— 1777 ½, 1, 2, 5 and 10 Kopecks.	5
469	— 1778 1, 2, 5 and 10 Kopecks.	4
470	— 1780 1, 2, 5 and 10 Kopecks.	4
471	Bactria, Parthia, Menander, Pantaleon, etc. Persia. 1 Shahi, 1273 = 1857 to present coinage, ½ and 1 Shahi, 1292–93, with several earlier, mostly with sun and lion. Fair to good.	25
472	Tabriz. 1239 = 1823 ½ and 1 Bisti. Face of sun in flames. Armenia. Leo II, 1181–1219 (2), Hethum I, 1223–69. Edessa. Bald. I or II, 1098–1118 (holed). Turkey in Asia. 1099–1687, Joffa. Jerusalem. Hotel checks for ½ and 1 Piastre, with others sim. in Greek, etc. Mostly fine. 17 to 29.	13
473	Hindostan. Coins of the Patan Kings, Native Princes and Mahomedan states of India. Many are thick. Unassorted, good to fine.	48
474	— Another asst. similar to preceding.	52
475	— Another, similar, the equal of either of the 2 preceding.	50
476	— Another selection, includes 8 that are square. Gd to fine.	27

477   Bengal. 1795–1817, Native inscriptions, ½ Pice, ¼, ½ Annas,
      also issues of 1825, '35, etc., to 1858, with East India
      Company's balemark, includes one in lead. Good to
      fine.   23

478   Bombay. 1741 (date defective) Dbl Pice. G R above cwn,
      below, BOMB. ℞ AUSPICIO etc. in 5 lines, also Pice of same
      design, without date. Fine, rare. Lead, 40, 33.   2

479   — 1 Pice (2), last century, no date, 1791–1834 Pie, ¼, ½
      Anna, 5, 10 and 20 Cash. Good to uncirculated, 1 a gilt
      proof.   15

480   Brit. India. 1862–78 $\frac{1}{12}$ to ½ Anna, all with bust of Victoria
      (9). Circars. 1794–97 $\frac{1}{96}$, $\frac{1}{48}$ Rupee (3), Indian amulet,
      a lead cast. Madras. C-C | E 17 | 55 etc., 20 Cash, 1803–8
      1, 5, 10, 20 do. Good to fine.   23

481   Mysore. 1218 (retrograde) = 1789–90 Elephant r., trunk
      raised; behind, a flag. ℞ Place of mintage in Persian. A
      very striking coin in perfect condition, dark olive. 34.   1

482   — Others, various mints. 2½, 5, 20 (3 var.) and 40 (2 var.)
      Cash, 1199–1222 = 1784–95. Elephants, trunk unraised,
      tail elevated on 2. V. good to fine.   7

483   — Others, still differing. 5 (2), 20 (4) and 40 (1) Cash. Fair
      to fine.   7

484   — Others, with elephant l. 10 (2), 20 and 40 Cash, from 3
      mints. Good to fine.   4

485   — Others, 5, 10 and 20 (4) Cash. Good to fine.   6

486   — Others, Elephant l., 5 (2), 20 (2) Cash; Lion l., 5 (3), 20
      (3) and 25 (1) do. Some dated 1834–49, others with Eng-
      lish value. Varied and choice; good to fine.   11

487   — Var. of the preceding. 5 (9), 20 (2), and 25 (2) Cash; 3
      with elephant, 5 with lion. Good to fine.   11

488   Oude. (1803–58) Dudu, ½ and 1 Paissa. Female stdg; mer-
      maids sup. crown, 2 females do., 2 lions do., also crown and
      fish within swords circled; dates and legends in Persian.
      Fair to good, mostly thick. 14 to 25.   18

489   Tranquebar. Fred. IV, D. O. C., 1 Cash; Fred. V, D. A. C.,
      4 do., etc. Pondicherry. ¼ Dudu, 1752, '53; 1 do., 1731,
      '52, '53, with 5 fleurs-de-lis; (1774–92) ½ and 1 Fanam, a large
      crown. ℞ 9 fleurs-de-lis. (1836) Dudu, new type. Good to
      fine; all scarce or rare. 13 to 30.   13

490 Portuguese-Asia. Peter II (?), 1668–1705 Arms. ℞ Cross.
Fon. 3888. Base, 21, 23. John V, 1705–50 and later, 6, 7½,
12, 15, 30 and 60 Reis, also ½ and 1 Tanga. Poor to good.
16½ to 37.   10

491 — Another asst. 6, 12 (?) and 60 Reis, ½ and 1 Tanga; also
a 60 Reis, 1811, CS. P R (script) | 809. Fon. 3931. Poor
to good. 18½ to 35.   7

492 — 1871 3, 5, 10, 15, 30, 60 Reis, INDIA PORTUG. Cwnd arms,
date. ℞ Value within wreath. Unc., light olive. 16 to 36.   6

493 — Damão. 1748, '68 12 Reis, both Æ, fair and good. 1801
15 do. D–O ℞ Date in angle of cross. Fine, lead. 33.
Also ½ Tanga, cwnd arms, M— ? Struck for Malacca. V.
fair. 27. All rare.   4

494 — Goa. ½, 1 Roda, n.d.; 10 Reis, 1769; 15 do., 1760, '69.
All in lead, with crowned arms, G—A. 1768 12 Reis. 1774
30 do. Both with G bet. date and value. Good to fine; all
rare.   9

495 Ceylon. Parakrama, 1153–86. Stdg figure. ℞ Kneeling
figure, bull, elephant, etc., E. I. Co. 1656–1796 ¼ Stvr., no
date. 1783 2 Stvrs. (thick). 1802 $\frac{1}{192}$, $\frac{1}{48}$ Rupee (gilt
proofs). 1815 ½, 1, 2 Stvrs. 1870 ¼, ½, 1 and 5 Cents.
Good to fine.   16

496 — 1787 1 Doit, bird on tree (lead, thick). Fine. $\frac{1}{48}$, $\frac{1}{24}$ and
$\frac{1}{12}$ Rupee, 1801–03. *Very* thick, poor and fair. (I have yet
to see fine specimens.) 1285=1869–70 An umbrella sup-
ported. ℞ Ins. and date. Good, lead. A Colombo token
for 18 Cents (an odd value, yet as certainly even). Fine,
brass. All rare.   6

497 Unattributed, all late, fine work, and doubtless rare; 2 bear
dates 1869 and 1870 in Arabic figures; some with Sanscrit
legends and inscriptions, others partly Arabic; one has face
of sun. Fine to unc. 21, 23 (2), 31, 32.   5

498 — Others, scarcely less interesting, though earlier, more pro-
nounced types (some with animals, one with sword), inferior
workmanship, and not as well preserved; includes one in
lead, size 39, round hole in centre.   22

499 Burmah. (Abt 1854) ½ Fuang. Peacock, and later, a lion *l.*,
same value, also rabbit *l.* (in lead). Pegu. $\frac{1}{10}$ Rupee, with
pentagonal hole in centre. Fon. 3772. Gd to fine. 21 to 25.   4

500 Siam. Maha Mongkut, 1851–58 $\frac{1}{16}$, $\frac{1}{8}$ (both lead), $\frac{1}{4}$ and $\frac{1}{2}$ Fuang. Chula-Longkorn, 1868 $\frac{1}{16}$ do. (lead). 1874 $\frac{1}{2}$, 1, 2 and 4 Att, the king's initial, cwnd. 1888 $\frac{1}{2}$ do., bust of the king. Mostly fine ; not a common piece in the lot. 20 to 38.   10

501 — Bangkok. Porcelain tokens issued by gambling houses under government protection. Two mandarins, lion with basket and blooming rose, in three and four colors. Perfect. 18 to 23$\frac{1}{2}$.   3

502 Malacca. 1 and 2 Kepeng. P. of W. Island. 1810, '25, '28 5 to 20 Cash (7). Straits Settlements. Sets of $\frac{1}{4}$, $\frac{1}{2}$ and 1 Cent, 1845, '62, '72, with others to 1877, $\frac{1}{4}$c. (1), 1 do. (4). Good to fine.   24

503 Cambodia. 1208=1846 Pattern $\frac{1}{4}$, $\frac{1}{2}$ and 3 Ticals. A pagoda. ℞ A hen posed l., legend and date in Cambodian. All with milled edges. Fon. 2159, 2161, 2163. Another, size of smallest, 4-line ins. within wreath on rev., edge plain. The largest shows slight handling ; the others are unc., brilliant. In white metal ; an extremely rare and very attractive set. 20 (2), 30, 44.   4

504 — A hen l. ℞ Plain. A base Fuang. Another, similar, better work, and Æ. Att. Fon. 2155, 2156. 1860 5, 10 Ctms, also tokens for the king's palace, 10, 15, 20, 25 Ctms, in brass. Fine to unc.   8

505 China. Knife Money, sometimes classed as razor-shaped. Tsih-moh. City of the Shantung peninsula, before B. C. 550. Very good ; nearly all characters distinct ; somewhat corroded. Length 7$\frac{1}{4}$ inches.   1

506 — Ming series, 317–228 B. C. Extreme points broken, otherwise good. 5$\frac{3}{4}$ in.   1

507 — Others as last, varying, each broken, though complete in parts. 5$\frac{1}{4}$ to 6$\frac{3}{8}$.   3

508 — Pu Money, spade-shaped, about 450 B. C. Fine. 25 x 45. Another, differently inscribed. Good. 28 x 47.   2

509 — Another, very fine. 31 x 52.   1

510 — Key-shaped. Wang-Mang, A. D. 9–72. Inscribed sim. to F. 1207. Very fine, and as an original, exceedingly rare. Length 2$\frac{1}{8}$ in.   1

511 — Another, similarly inscribed, larger characters ; planchet thin, when compared with the preceding. Fine, v. rare. 2$\frac{7}{8}$.   1

512 **China.** New Pu Money, inscribed sim. to Fon. 1199. Fine,
rare. 22 x 57. 1

513 — Round Money, square hole in centre, 246–209 B. C. Fon.
1185 (2 var.), and 2 others. 25 to 35. 4

514 — Others, all named according to numbers in Fon. Cat., from
A. D. 9–72 to epoch Hi-Ning, 1067–77. Fair to fine. 20½
to 29½. 39

515 — Others, 1067–77 to epoch Kjan-Yan, 1131–62. Arranged
as last. Mostly fine. 23 to 35. 42

516 — Others, 1131–62 to 1505–21. Arranged as last. Mostly
fine. 22½ to 32. 46

517 — Others, 1525–21 to 1661–1772. Arranged as last. Good
to fine. 22 to 28. 43

518 — Others, 1661–1772 to 1796–1820. 1 Cash. Arranged as
last. Good to fine. 45

519 — Others, 1820–50. 1 to 10 Cash, 17, together with 7 numbered by Neumann. Good. 15 to 35. 26

520 — The larger sort. Epoch Tschi-tsching, 1341–68. 10 Cash.
Epoch Ta-tschung, 1368. 5 Cash. Fine. 45, 39. 2

521 — Epoch Hung-Wu, 1368–98. 10 Cash. Fon. 1516. 2
marked varieties. Fine. 42, 45½. 2

522 — Tsching-te, 1505–21. Dragon and Paradise bird. ℞
"Tsching-te-tung-pao." 2, 5 and 10 Cash. Fon. 1536, 1540,
1542. Fine. 29, 31, 48½. 3

523 — Tao-kwang, 1820–50. Proclamation 5 Cash. "Tao-kwang-
tung-pao." Floral attachments to the usual circular design, above (with loop) and below. Fon. 1714. Fine.
35 x 78. 1

524 — Same period. 5 Cash. Pieces lapped and joined. Fon.
1715. Fine. 36 x 65. 1

525 — Hjan-fung, 1850–61. 5, 10, 50 and 100 Cash. Last 3 ac-
companied by Fon. descriptions, 1751, 1760, 1780. Fine.
28, 37, 45, 60. 4

526 — Others, varying mints. 10 Cash (2 sizes, one in iron), 50
do. (2 sizes). Fon. 1753, 1754, 1759, 1783. Fine. 31 to 52. 5

527 — Others, 10 Cash (4 mints) and 50 do. Good to fine. 33
(2), 37, 44, 45. 5

528 — Others, 50 Cash, Pekin mint and another from Su-tscheu-fu,
Province of Kjang-su. Fon. 1750, 1781. Fine. 56, 54. 2

529 **China.** 100 Cash, minted at Su-tscheu-fu, Prov. of Kjang-su.
Fon. 1780. Fine. 58.   1
530 Thung-tschi. 1861–75 Proclamation 5 Cash and others. Fon.
1789, 1794. Also 10 Cash, Pekin. Good to fine. 23 to 31.   3
531 Unattributed. First 3 early. 34, 38, 39, 45, 48, 51, the last
with small deer ? Good to fine.   6
532 Various unassorted Cash, some early, mostly very good.   80

TEMPLE MONEY.

533 Shield-shape, surface in tiled form, characters and figures;
holed in centre; mended on back, which is plain. Fine.
48 x 75.   1
534 Pear-shaped. Animals and characters on both sides. Die-
projecting loop. Fon. 1980. V. good. 51 x 72.   1
535 Wreath-form, branches depending from die-projecting loop,
piece of Cash imbedded in centre. Fine. 49 x 65.   1
536 Apple-shaped, characters obv. and rev. Stem with leaves form
loops. Fine. 28 x 40.   1
537 *Round.* 12 signs of the Zodiac outside of Grecian border,
within, characters in circle, around hole in centre. ℞ A
robed male figure from which two smaller ones are fleeing.
Fon. 1896. V. good. 71.   1
538 Two dragons. Open work, round hole in centre. Fon. 1991.
Good. 59.   1
539 Another, similar. Fon. 1992. 50.   1
540 Others, similar. Fruits and leaves. 54. Flowers and leaves.
46. Both good.   2
541 A crane and flowers. ℞ Characters in circle, round hole. V.
good. 46. Man *r.*, characters *l.* ℞ As last. Fine. 44.
Fon. 1964, 1965.   2
542 12 animals around border, 12 characters within, encircling
round hole. ℞ Characters and clusters of lines. Fon. 1897.
V. good. Sizes 43, 46. Another, 16 characters around border, 8 within. ℞ Same arrangement of different characters.
Fon. 1930. Fine. 48.   3
543 Characters in 7 perpendicular lines. ℞ Characters and clusters of lines. 44. Quadrupeds and fish. ℞. 2 fishes and
2 characters. 23½. Both good, round holes.   2

544 Robed male stdg. ℞ Horse and cow. Holed near edge.
Man stdg beside frame (twice holed near edge), and 2 others
with characters only (Fon. 1900, 1933). All without the
usual hole in centre. Good. 23 to 29. 4

545 *Square hole* in centre to end of series. Fishes and birds. ℞
Characters, cross form, Grecian borders, piece broken from
edge. Fine. 46. Stag and tree. ℞ Characters in cross
form, Grecian border. Good. 52. 2

546 Dragons. ℞ Characters, cross form. 54. Characters in circle. ℞ Plain field. 54. Good. 2

547 Dragons? ℞ Clusters of lines (pc from edge), another as first
in lot 543, and 2 having characters only (Fon. 1918, 1924).
Good to fine. 43 to 45. 4

548 Small and large male figure, turtle, serpent, etc. Others, male
figure, pot of flowers, etc. Fon. 1947, 1949, 1952. V. good.
32 to 41. 3

549 Deity, lamb and bird (holed), seven busts and four couples
embracing. Good. 27 to 28½. 3

550 Robed male *l.*; horse and rider *l.*; female and bird; man leading horse. Good to fine. 32½ to 37. 4

551 Horse *l.* (4). Horse *r.* (3). Rooster and scales? All but
one have characters on rev. Good to fine. 9

552 Lizards, dragons, daggers, and various others with characters
only. 12 have Fon. numbers accompanying. Good to
fine. 21

553 Hong-Kong. Mills, 1863–66 (3). Cents, 1863–77 (6). Co-
chin China. 1879 Sepeque and Cent. Corea. 10 Mun
(value in English), and 10 others of same value, native inscription. Fine to unc. 22

554 Japan. Epoch, Ho-yei, 1704–10. 10 Sen, size 37; other Sen,
unassorted, early and late, characters generally upon one side
only. Fair to fine. 34

555 Loo-Choo Islands. ½ Sjn. Fon. 1110. Fine. 42. 1

OCEANICA.

556 Sumatra. 1787 1, 2 and 3 Kepangs, bronzed proofs. 1798 3
do., a gilt proof. 1804 1, 2 and 4 Kepangs. Acheen. Kuh,
in lead. Good to fine. 7

557 Jambi. Lead, with round hole in centre (2), 1 dated 1300= 1881. Pelembang. Similar. Fon. 827, also in lead. Java. Temple money. 2 male figures. ℞ Horse *l.* Another, with 2 females. Fon. 337. 1 fair, others good to unc. 19 to 40.   5

558 Java. Under the Dutch. 1799, 1800 1 Stvr. 1807 Doit, with V. O. C. Under the French. 1809, '10 Doits; 1810 ½ Stvr. Under the English E. I. Co. 1811–14 ½ Str. (3), 1 do., and 1 Doit, in lead. Batavia. 1644 ½ Stvr., sword erect. Fair to good. 20 to 33½.   12

559 — Under the Dutch E. I. Co. Arms of Holland. ½ Doit, 1750, '53; Doits, 1731–92 (18). Overyssel. ½ Doit, 1788, '89; Doits, 1731–86 (12). Utrecht. Doits, 1753–94; dbl do., 1790 (15). West Frisia. Doits, 1729–92 (21). Zeeland. ½ Doit, 1789; Doits, 1727–94 (18). Good to fine.   84

560 India — Batavia, various. ½ and 1 Doit and ½ Stvr., 1804–1825, including an obv. impression of 1816 in lead. Good to fine.   24

561 Netherlands, Ind. ⅛, ¼, ½ Stvrs., 1822–26; 1 and 2 Cents, 1833–40. Mints J. S. V. and W. Good.   30

562 — Last issue. ½ Cent, 1856 to '60, all unc., red; 1 do., 1855 (proof), 1857 to '60; 2½ do., 1856 (proof), '57. Good to fine.   12

563 Celebes Is. Kepang. Hen. ℞ 16-ptd star. Bonton Is. (near Celebes). Piece of cotton cloth, 1¾ x 3½, used as currency. Fine.   2

564 British No. Borneo. ½ Cent, 1886, '91; Cent, 1886, '88, '90, '91. Labuk Planting Co., 20, 50c., $1.00. Labuk, British No. Borneo, same values. Sandakan Tobacco Co., 10, 20, 50c. and $1.00. Soengy Diskie Estate, 50c. and $1.00. Every piece in the lot unc., bright red. 19 to 38.   18

565 Sarawak. J. Brooke, 1863, ¼, ½ and 1 Cent; C. Brooke, 1870, same values, also Cent of 1879. Unc. 4, others good to fine.   7

566 Sultana Is. 1804 Kepang. Philippine Is. Ferd. VII, Quartos, 1820, '29, '34; 1859 pattern 20 Reaux, and an imposition of same date for 2 Cts. Hawaii. 1847 Cent, also 2 very rare tokens by W. P. for VI and 12½ Cents, 1871. H I above 5-ptd star; 10 stars around border. Fair to unc.   9

567 Australian Tradesmen's Copper Tokens. Probably the most complete collection ever offered for sale, publicly or privately, including 298 of the 305 described by Mr. Stainsfield, whose own collection was purchased and merged into the one here offered, several years ago. There are also 10 pieces I do not find in Stainsfield, some of which have been issued since his work was published. The condition is generally fine ; 2 are holed. 308

MISCELLANEOUS.

568 Florida. Jas. II, 1685–88 $\frac{1}{24}$ Real, pewter. Specimens from different dies. V. fair and good. Sizes 26, 28. New Jersey. Cent, 1788, Fox type. Fair. 3

569 Penn. or Bungtown Halfpence, including Washington. ℞ North Wales. Fair to good. 21

570 St. Bartholomew. Crown CS. on Cayenne Sou. Mexico. 1832 $\frac{1}{16}$ Real. Cent. Am. Union. 1889 1 and 2 Ctvs., impositions. Pernambuco. 1697, '99 20 Reis. Peru. Mine token for 20c., etc. Fair to fine. 9

571 England. Farthing Tokens by merchants. Liverpool, London, Norwich, Manchester, and various small places. A few early (after Conder's period), but mostly in time of Victoria up to 1852 ; includes Kirk's Penny Token, in brass, "In St. Pauls | Church | Yard." Good to fine. 75

572 — Cards of merchants, and tokens, checks, and tickets of value of public houses, collieries, places of entertainment, etc. Chiefly late, and in brass. Mostly unc. ; some sets ; a few odd shapes ; many large. 156

573 Scotland. Tokens, chiefly Glasgow, including Halfpenny size by John Wright, in brass, but mostly Farthings, and prior to Victoria. Good to fine. 22

574 France. Merchants' cards, etc., one referring to balloon and pigeon service during siege of 1870. Spain. Barcelona, Valencia, etc. Mostly brass, 2 Decagon. Good to fine. 15

575 Alcmaar ? Large A | 8 ℞ Lion, Amsterdam 1789 R. B. Also Workhouse Tokens for 10, 25, 50c., Antwerp, 1551, open hand, cwnd. Bishop Wellens, 1823 ; Daventer, 1654 ; Linen-weavers, Leyden, (15)74, etc. Æ, brass and lead. Good to fine. 10

576 Maestricht. 1682 Carpenters' Guild Token, used at funerals.
Utrecht. Bust. ℞ Arms. Holland. L. Nap. 1808 Pat.
20 Gulden. Danzig. 1771 ℞ 3 crowns, Poorhouse Token.
Andorra. 1875 10 Ctmos (imposition). Hedwigsburg. 2
and 4 Quartiers, obv. impressions, mandarin and attendant,
etc. Good to fine.   12

577 Money weights for testing gold coins, 17th and 18th centuries.
Chiefly Italian, many Genoese and Papal ; a few with bust,
but mostly arms. Some large and thick, a few in odd shapes.
Good to fine.   86

578 Spielmarks, unassorted (40), and a few odds and ends of coins,
etc., some curious (18). Fair to fine.   58

VARIETIES AND UNASSORTED DUPLICATES OF COPPER COINS AND TOKENS.

⁎ Some of the following are in choice condition, while many are the equal
of those which precede them.

579 **England.** *Penny Tokens*, 18th century (Conder's period).
Anglesey. 1787 5 (1 with D1 above cipher, Conder, 3/15,
a proof). 1788 (8) Halsall ; Birmingham (Co.), Hereford,
etc. Good to fine.   20

580 Chester. Conder, 22/1, unc. ; Bath, 130/1, plain edge (dent-
ed) ; Birm. Co., 160/1, unc. ; Gloucester, 313/17, proof. 3
rare.   4

581 *Halfpennies.* Anglesey, 5/29 ; Southampton, 43/26 ; Ibber-
son's, 89/163 ; Bath, 133/23 (milled edge, *brass*) ; No. Wales,
155/3 (dif. edge) ; British, 211/15 (in copper) ; End of Pain,
232/188. Good to proof.   7

582 Bishop Blaze, 269/46 (not previously catalogued, omitted
from lot 56, where page is erroneously given 369 instead of
269) ; Fox, 277/34 ; Oppression, 288/240. (All unc.) 288/242.
V. good.   4

583 Oppression, 288/244 ; Thelwall, 297/344, 298/347, also rev.
Minerva, "Truth for my helm," etc. (good) ; Tree of Liberty, 299/359 ; Turnstile, 300/375. Unc.   6

584 Various. All different, unc., light olive to bright red.   16

585 Another assortment, in same condition.   18

586 Unassorted, mostly good to fine, as are also the 7 following
lots.   42

587 Another. 42
588 Another. 42
589 Another. 42
590 Another. 42
591 Another. 42
592 Another. 42
593 Another, includes 11 Penn. or Bungtowns. 25
594 *Farthings.* Dundee, 13/13 16; Essex Co., 35/12; Denton, 114/36. All rarities. Fine to unc. 4
595 Glorious Duncan, 247/27; Industry, 250/48; London, 114/357; Bath, 138/62; and a duplicate of Dundee, 13/16. Good to unc. 5
596 Shop cards, late, in brass, same as in 572 (23), Sweden, Luxemburg, France (essai 1792), Spain and Portugal. Mostly good to fine. 51
597 **Italy.** Various cities, principalities, etc., 13th to 15th century (72). Nap. I and Vic. Em. II. Mostly fair to good. 98
598 Ancona, Aquila (13), Ascoli, Bologna (35), Brindisi, Cagliari (3), Castro, Chieti (2). Fair to good. 58
599 Correggio, Etruria (3), Fano, Fermo (6), Ferrara (39). Mostly fair to good. 50
600 Fuligno, all Pius VI (4); Genoa, 1768–1814 (18); Gorlitz, 1733–99, ½ to the large 3 Soldi (9); Gubbio, Benedict XIII to Pius VI, Quat. to 2½ Bai., several large (30). Fair to good. 61
601 Lombardy-Venice, 1 to 10 Ctmi (22); Lucca and Lucca-Piombino, mostly 1806-26 (18, 6 with conjoined busts); Mantua, Ferd. II, 1519-30 to siege (1799), several with bust of Virgilius Maro (30). Mostly fair to good, a few very choice. 70
602 Massa (2); Milan, Chas. V, 1535-55, to M. Theresa, 1777 (28); Mirandola (4); Modena (6); Monaco, Hy. IV, 5 and 10 Ctms (13, including 2 patterns by *Rogat*); Montalto (2); Orbetello (3); Parma (13). Mostly fair to good. 71
603 Naples and Sicily. Roger II, 1102–54 to Francis II, 1859. A very extensive selection. Mostly good, as are also the 2 following lots. 92
604 Another selection, covering the same period. 80
605 Another, answering same description. 66

606 Others, Roger II to Phil. III, 1556–98 (26) ; Naples, Hy. of
    Lorraine, 1648, 1, 2 and 3 Tornesi (12) ; Naples, Republic
    (1799), 4 and 6 Tornesi (10) ; Perugia, 2½ Bai., Pius VI (5);
    Pesaro (7) ; Piedmont, Presiaü (3) ; Ragusa (5). Mostly
    fair to good.   68
607 Papal. Clement VIII, 1592–1605, to Pius IX, 1846–78. Many
    large. Mostly very good.   49
608 Others, Urban VIII, 1623–44, to Pius IX. A very similar
    asst. in same condition.   39
609 Others, Alex. VII, 1655–67 to Pius IX. Similar to last.   35
610 Others, Paul II, 1464–71 to Benedict XIV, 1740–58, including
    coinages of 17 Popes. Quat. and ½ Bai. Many good.   54
611 Ravenna (7), Reggio (4), Roman Rep. (1799), including the
    rare one with 3 fasces in triangle, all 2 Bai. (13), 1849 1 and
    3 Bai. (6).   37
612 Rome. Clem. XII, 1730–49 to Greg. XVI, 1831–46 Quat., ½,
    1, 2 and 2½ Bai. Mostly good, many large.   54
613 Sardinia (27), Savoy (4), Sienna (6), Tivoli, Tuscany (16), Ur-
    bino (8), Viterbo (11). Fair to very good.   73
614 Venice. Many different Doges. Mostly early.   90
615 Russia. Cath. I, 1726 5 Kopecks. Dbl-hd eagle within dotted
    circle, sep. date. ℞ Blank. *Restrike.* V. fine, brilliant.
    42 x 42.   1
616 1726 10 Kopecks. Arms within dotted circle in the 4 corners,
    value and date in centre. ℞ Blank. *Restrike.* Very fine,
    brilliant. 62 x 62. A duplicate of this brought $10.25 in
    Part I.   1
617 An extensive assortment of ¼, ½, 1, 2, 5 and 10 Kopecks, from
    Peter the Great to Nicholas I ; the larger pieces predominate
    and include some of the heaviest circular copper coins struck
    in any country. Mostly very good, some are rare.   143
618 A similar lot, selected to be the equal of the preceding.   128
619 Another lot, answering the same description.   119
620 Catharine II, 5 Kopecks, various dates and mints, A–M
    (8), C II–M (2), K–M (11), M–M (4). Many good to
    fine.   25
621 1796 Pattern 4, 5 and 10 Kopecks. E II cwnd, dots around
    border indicate value, also ½ Kop., 1765. Edges diagonally
    milled, all very choice, partly bright. 22 to 47.   4

622 Poland (15), Moldavia-W. (3), Turkey (5), Crimea (5, two v. large), Greece (20). Fair to fine.   48

623 Armata (4), Dalmatia (2), Candia (7), Corfu, Cyprus (3), Congo (4, set), Egypt (10), Morocco (5), Oran (3), Terceira, Tripoli (5), Tunis (10), Zanzibar, and 4 bright red impositions. Fair to unc.   60

624 Siberia. Cath. II. Sables support arms. $\frac{1}{4}$, $\frac{1}{2}$, 1, 2, 5 and 10 Kopecks. 2 complete sets. Fine to unc.   12

625 Three more sets. Fine.   18

626 Four more sets. Fine.   24

627 Others, $\frac{1}{2}$ Kop. (4), 1 do. (7), 2 do. (12), 5 do. (10), 10 do. (17), of the last, some have lettered edge. Mostly good to fine.   50

628 Tiflis, with cwn (2), Persia, lion, sun, etc. (8), Bengal (9), Cambodia, Ceylon (4), Malacca (6), Siam, Æ and tin (4), etc. Mostly good to fine.   37

629 Straits Settlements (2), Tranquebar (3), China, various, some 10 and 50 Cash, Temple money, etc., none common (18). Good to fine, 1 holed. 27 to 55.   24

630 Ind. Batavia (11), Java, V. O. C., etc. (19), Nedl. Ind. (9), Labuk (3), Sandakan (4), Sarawak (3), Sumatra (4), Palembang (2), Philippines (2), Australian Tokens (7), Hawaii, etc. Many good to fine.   65

631 Australian Tradesmen's Tokens. Halfpennies (12), Pennies (29). All different. Good to fine, 1 holed.   41

632 A varied lot, consisting of overflows, out of sight, misplaced, etc., chiefly Italian. Fair to good.   65

633 The poor and holed, contains some rare pieces.   287

634 **Base Coins.** Unassorted, chiefly Italian, some large and very fine, including one of John Jacob of Viglevano, 1500–18. Arms. ℞ St. George. In good condition. Size 28. Mostly fair to good.   126

635 **Silver Coins.** England. Commonwealth, 1653 Shilling. V. good. Also 2d. Good.   2

636 Sweden. Eric, 1395–1459 Ortug for Stockholm. Mantua. Bust of Virgilius Maro. ℞ Sun. Wm. Gonzaga, 1550–87. V. good. 18, 14, 15.   3

636a Denmark. Fred. III, 1659 4 Marks. Hand reaching for cwn, severed by sword in hand from cloud. V. L. II, 431. Fine. Æ 41.   1

637 Sydney, Australia. 3 Pence by Hogarth and Erichsen, 1860.
Stainsfield 15. Good, very rare.   1

MEDALS.

Æ Silver. Æ Bronze.

638 Washington, St. Gaudens' bust *l*. ℞ 12 line inscription. Loop
and bar ins. 1789 — New York | G W — 1889. Given to
Committee of 100. About perfect, very rare. Æ 35.   1
639 Mexico. Chas. IV, 1789 Proclamation medal, with incorrect
obvs. From Fischer sale. Very fine. Æ 40.   3
640 Ferd. VII, War Medal ? ℞ Yzquier da 2. A. 4. Circular hole
in centre. Essai. 8 Rls. Obv. by *Kurtz*. Max., 1863 As-
sembly of notables. Good to fine. Æ 34, 37, 20.   3
641 Campeche. 1790 Procl. 2 Rls. Original. Edge o☐o Fis.
608. Good. Puebla. 1790 with Campeche rev. Santiago
de Tuxtla. 1809 with Mexico and New Santander revs.
Size of 8 Rls. About perfect. All Æ.   4
642 Oaxaca. Chas. IV, 1789 Procl. 2 Rls. Original. Edge o☐o
Fis. 480. Perfect. 27. Toluca, 1822. Fis. 364. Lima, 1877,
burning of Bank bills. Cat. 4, 657. Both fine. Brazil, Jeton.
Fon. 8676. Buenos Ayres, 1854 (holed). Good. All Æ.   5
643 Pasquaro. Ferd. VII, 1808 Procl. Medals, with obvs. of Chas.
IV and Ferd. VII, of Mexico, New Santander and Zamora.
All about perfect, partly bright. Æ 42.   4
644 England. Jas. I, 1604 Peace with Spain. Bust in hat, cwnd.
JACOBVS . D . G . ANG . SCO . etc. A — S engraved in field. ℞
Peace and Religion stdg. *Ex.* date. Open-work border.
Orig. cast, chased. M. I. 14, Van Loon II, 19. Æ, size 40. 1
645 — Chas. I (1649), Memorial. Bust *r*. ℞ VIRTVT . EX . ME .
etc., hand from cloud with cwn. M. I. 200, V. L. II, 320.
About perfect. Æ 51.   1
646 — Chas. II (1667), Peace of Breda. CAROLVS . SECVNDVS . DEI .
GRATIA MAG . BRI . etc. Hd *r*. ℞ FAVENTE DEO Britannia
setd *l*. *Ex.* BRITANNIA M. I. 186, V. L. II, 522. Several
edge dents, otherwise good, rare. Æ 56.   1
647 — Wm. and Mary, 1689, Festivities at Rotterdam. M. I. 55,
V. L. III, 391. Size 30. Anne, 1702, Coronation. M. I.
4, V. L. IV, 347. Perfect, brilliant. 34. 1706, Battle of
Ramilies. M. I. 92, V. L. V, 33. V. fine. 34. All Æ.   3

648 England. Medalets. Kirk series (12, Cromwell in duplicate), Col. Noel (inscriptions only), Corunna, etc. in 6 lines, 42 | R. H. R.ᵀ, Nelson and others. 6 in brass, remainder Æ. Good to fine, 2 holed as issued.   25

649 Netherlands. (1572), Harlem, Invention of printing. 31. Tergou, Counsellor's medal, view of the city. 31. (1573) Alcmar, raising of siege. 33. V. L. I, 158, 149, 166. Fine to about perfect. Æ.   3

650 — 1574, Leyden. Necessity coin for 20 Sols. GODT BEHOEDE etc. R⁄ Lion with Liberty pole sep. date. V. L. I, 180. V. good. 37 x 37.   1

651 — (1574) Leyden. Commemorating the raising of the siege of the city. Van Loon I, 193. Distinct varieties. Æ 30.   2

652 — 1574, Leyden. Retreat of the Spaniards before the city. View of the city, soldiers in flight. V. L. I, 193. Fine. Æ 46.   1

653 — 1594, Siege of Groningen. CONSULIBUS JOH: etc. Soldier in armor, stdg. R⁄ Ins. in 11 lines (8 in script). Abt perfect. Æ 48.   1

654 — 1594, Maurice of Nassau. Groningen reunited to the States. View of army before city. R⁄ AB ASSERTIS | SIBI SECVNDVM | etc. in 12 lines. V. L. I, 440. Fine. Æ 51.   1

655 — 1602, Maurice of Nassau. Capture of Grave. ARS. GRAVE. TOLLIT etc. R⁄ INDVSTRIA. ET. LABORE V. L. I, 552. V. fine. Æ 48.   1

656 — 1648, Peace with Spain. Female with Mercury's wand, in chariot drawn by 2 lions. R⁄ PACIS FŒLICITAS | etc. in 9 lines. V. L. II, 301. Very good. 58.   1

657 — 1650, On the death of Wm. II, turning into ridicule his project against Amsterdam. CRIMINE AB UNO etc. Horse leaping l. R⁄ MAGNIS EXCIDIT etc. View of the city. Horses broken from chariot on clouds above. V. L. II, 341. A slight edge dent, otherwise about perfect, brilliant. Æ 68.   1

658 — 1666, Alchemical Medal. OPERÆ PRO ARIS etc. Alchemist setd before fire-place. R⁄ ARGENTVM EX FVMO etc. In field 9 line inscription. V. L. II, 516. V. fine. Æ 57.   1

659 Netherlands, 1672, Cornelius and John DeWitt. Their busts
vis-a-vis. ℞ NUNC REDEUNT ANIMIS etc. Ravenous animals
devouring two nude prostrate figures. In memory of the
brothers — Burgomaster and Minister of State — assassi-
nated by the mob at the Hague. V. L. III, 81. Fine.
Æ 71.   1

660 — 1672, Siege of Groningen July 9th, raised Aug. 17th. Army
in field, three roads leading to walled city, above, DEI VIRTVTE
PROCERVM etc. ℞ GRONINGA · | A COLONIENSI etc. in 16
lines. V. L. III, 94. Fine. Æ 58.   1

661 — 1672. Obv. type of last, without legend. ℞ SIT SVMMA
etc. In field, ANNO | CIƆ IƆ CLXXII etc. in 10 lines. V. L.
III, 94. V. fine. Æ 56.   1

662 — 1672, Same occasion. Mural tablet and pillars, city arms
within, Mars stdg above amid his attributes. ℞ IN | MEMO-
RIAM | OBSIDIONIS · etc. in 9 lines. V. L. III, 96. V. good.
Æ 46½.   1

663 — 1672, Obv. sim. to 661. In l. field, BELEGERINGE | VOOR |
GRONINGEN ℞ COEVERDEN . MET . etc. Soldiers surround
7-bastioned fort. Coevorde taken by storm Dec. 20th. V.
L. III, 103. V. fine. Æ 54.   1

664 — 1672, Obv. as last. ℞ CRO · IS · BELE · etc. A different
view of Coevorde. V. L. III, 104. Fine. Æ 53.   1

665 — 1696, MOTOS PRÆSTAT etc. Neptune in car r. ℞ HALCY-
ONIBVS REDVCTIS | etc. in 5 lines on scroll above sea. 2
chickens in small open boat. V. L. IV, 221. To the Bour-
geoisie and Volunteers of Amsterdam for quelling insurrection. About perfect. 38. Another. Fine, a few nicks.
Æ 49.   2

666 — 1696, Another, same as the smaller piece in the next preceding. Nearly fine. Also an exact duplicate of No. 663. Æ. 2

667 — 1697, Same occasion. S. C. PRÆF. CIV. etc. ℞ URBI QUAS-
SATÆ. Soldiers dispersing mob before public building. V. L.
IV, 222. V. fine. W.m. 55. 1702, ANTIQUA etc., lion l. with
Liberty pole. ℞ FRANGIMUR SI COLLIDIMUR (We break if
we clash). 7 bowls floating on open sea. V. L. IV, 35.
About perfect. Æ 34.   2

   This is the origin of the famous device of the floating jars used on Continental Paper Money, during the Revolution. See Betts, p. 248.

668 Netherlands. Jetons, 1512–88. Numbered according to Neumann on Copper coins. Fair to fine. 50

669 — 1587–1619, Another lot, sim. to preceding. 50

670 — 1624–67, Another. 50

671 — 1664–97, and a few without date. 58

672 — Another lot mostly late, several of Namur, Belgium, etc. Many fine to bright red, including a small Catholic medalet, with legend in Chinese characters. 34

674 France. Jetons and medalets, 17th to 19th century. Mostly good to fine. Æ and brass. 41

675 Spain. Louis I, 1724 Proclamation Medal for Granada. Bust of the King. ℞ Pomegranate. Fine, rare. Brass 29. 1

676 Germany. Chas. VI, 1711 Coronation at Frankfort. Æ 18, 26. Another referring to his election. W.m. 48. V. L. V, 190, 196. Augsburg. 1706 (in chronogram) Religious Festival. Æ 30 x 30; and a Belgian R. R. Medal, 1843. Æ 27. V. fine. 5

677 Hamburg. 1686 Vainly besieged. NON OMNIA TERRENTIA etc. View of city. ℞ Eagles attacking sheep. V. L. IV, 323. V. good, holed. Æ 48. 1

678 Eckernförde. 1848 War Medal (in brass). Fair. Size 22. Others, Medalets. Gern, 1850 (holed); Hallberg, 1828; Frankfort, n.d., " Dem | Fleisse"; Saalfield, 1832, School. Good to fine. Æ. 5

679 Sardinia, 1746; Russia, 1725–1842 (12, only 2 of present century), Jetons and Medalets. Mostly in fine preservation. Æ 20 to 32. 13

680 Bulgaria. 1887, '89 Jetons of Ferd. and Alex. (3), and others, several religious. Fair to fine, mostly Æ 18 to 31. 18

681 Persia. 1873, etc. Bust of Shah r., Æ 28; l. and facing, brass 23, perfect; also lion setd r., sun behind, Persian ins. in 2 lines below, fine. W.m. 35. 4

NUMISMATIC BOOKS.

682 Akerman, J. Y. Tradesmen's Tokens Current in London and its vicinity, between the years 1648 and 1672. 257 pp., 8 plates. 8vo, cloth. London, 1849. 1

683 Burn, Jacob Henry. A Descriptive Catalogue of the London
Traders, Tavern and Coffee-House Tokens current in the
Seventeenth Century. 237 pp. 8vo, cloth. London,
1853.   1

684 Cinagli, Dr. Angelo. Le Monete de' Papi descritte in Tavole
Sinnotiche. 480 pp., 4 plates. Folio, half calf. Fermo,
1848.   1

685 Conder, James. An arrangement of Provincial Coins, Tokens
and Medalets issued in Great Britain, Ireland and the Colonies within the last twenty years. 330 pp., 3 plates. Small
8vo, half morocco. Rare. A copy that has passed through
the hands of owners of several large collections, and also
bearing Colonel Cutting's check throughout. Ipswich,
1799.   1

686 — Another copy, 1798, and a remarkably clean one — bears
only one check covering but a small ground. Half calf.   1

687 Crosby, S. S. Early Coins of America, comprising Mass. Pine
Tree money, the Washington Pieces, Anglo-American To-
kens, First Patterns of the U. S. Mints. 381 pp., 10 plates.
Large 4to, half morocco. Boston, 1878.   1

688 Denton, M. The Virtuoso's Companion and Coin Collector's
Guide. Containing 180 plates illustrating obverse and reverse of 720 English Tokens, with an index of same. Preceding Mr. Conder's work and covering the same ground.
2 Vols. 8vo, Small half calf. London, 1795-6. Very
rare.   2

689 Fleurimont, G. R. Medailles du Règne de Louis XV. 77
handsome engravings, each with description of the Medal,
within beautifully designed borders. Folio, calf. Front
cover detached.   1

690 Fonrobert, Jules. Catalogue of his Collection of Coins and
Medals, North America, Mexico, Central America, West
India Islands, South America, Africa, Asia and Australia.
1575 pp., covering descriptions of upwards of 16,000 lots.
Numerous illustrations throughout the text, with 44 plates
in Vol. III. 3 Vols. Large 8vo, half morocco. Text in
German. Berlin, 1877-8. (Printed prices of all except Vol.
III.) One of the most valuable catalogues or text-books
for the countries named. Rare.   3

Frossard, E. Monograph of United States Cents and Half Cents, issued between the years 1793 and 1857. 58 pp., 9 plates. 4to, half morocco. 1879.   1

Gandolfi, G. C. Della Moneta Antica di Genova. 298 pp. and plate. 8vo, half calf. Genoa, 1841.   1

Gnecchi, F. ed E. Le Monete di Milano da Carlo Magno a Vittorio Emanuel II, with preface by Bernado Biondelli. xcv and 256 pp., 18 plates. Folio, cloth. Milan, 1884.   1

Lane-Poole, Stanley. The Coins of the Sultans of Delhi, in the British Museum. xliv and 199 pp., with 11 plates and map. 8vo, cloth, in fine condition. London, 1884.   1

— The Coins of the Mohammedan States of India, in the British Museum. lxx and 239 pp., with 12 plates and map. 8vo, cloth, in fine condition. London, 1885.   1

Laskey, J. C. Medals of Napoleon Bonaparte. Large 8vo, boards. 239 pp. London, 1818.   1

Leroux, Jos., M. D. Le Medaillier du Canada. (The Canadian Coin Cabinet.) 308 pp., with index. Every coin illustrated. Large 8vo, cloth. Montreal, 1888.   1

Maris, Dr. Edward. A Historic Sketch of the Coins of New Jersey, with plate containing specimens of Mark Newbie's coppers and the issues of 1786-7-8, etc. 16 pp. Large folio, cloth. Philadelphia, 1881.   1

Menestrier, Claude F. Histoire du Roy Louis le Grand. 54 pp., with several engravings of coats of arms of French Orders of nobility and military.— Also 37 plates illustrating medals. Small folio, boards. An interesting work. Paris, 1693.   1

Millies, H. C. Recherches sur les Monnaies des Indigènes de l'Archipel Indien et de la Peninsule Malaie. 179 pp., 26 plates. Folio, half morocco. Handsomely printed. The Hague, 1871.   1

Neumann, Josef. Beschreibung der bekanntesten Kupfermünzen. 6 Vols. 2482 pp., 79 plates. 8vo, boards. Text in German. As a reference book it is unequalled, describing upwards of 40,000 Coins. European price commonly 100 Marks, and not often appearing complete. Prague, 1858-72.   6

Reiske, Jacob. Briefe über das Arabische Munzwesen. 362 pp., text in German with Arabic legends. Small 8vo, boards. Leipzig, 1781.   1

703 Rentzmann, William. Numismatisches Legenden-Lexicon des Mittelalters und der Neuzeit. Giving a list of Kings, Princes and Rulers, with dates of reign, patron saints, and the places to which they belong, with old Latin names of places, etc., etc. 293 pp., including supplement. 8vo, half morocco. Berlin, 1865.   1

704 Rigollot and Leber. Monnaies inconnues des Evêques des Innocens, des Fous, etc. 218 pp., and illustrations of 119 different Coins, Tokens, etc. 8vo, half morocco. Paris, 1837.   1

705 Rouyer, J. and Hucher, E. Histoire du Jeton au Moyen age. 177 pp., 17 plates illustrating 149 Coins. Large 8vo, half morocco. Paris, 1858.   1

706 Ruding, Rev. Rogers. Annals of the Coinage of Great Britain and its Dependencies. 6 Vols. 2413 pp. Boards. Vols. I to V, 8vo ; Vol. VI, folio, containing the plates (82). London, 1819.   6

707 Russian Gold, Silver and Copper Coins, with extensive and accurate tables of the different coinages in each metal — from Peter the Great to Alexander II, with mint-marks, moneyers, etc. In Russian. Small 4to, half morocco. St. Petersburg, 1883.   1

708 Sandham, Alfred. Coins, Tokens and Medals of the Dominion of Canada. 83 pp., 9 plates. 8vo, half morocco. The copy presented by the author, with autograph letter, to Mr. Chas. I. Bushnell. Montreal, 1869.   1

709 Schubert, Genl. T. F. de. Monnayes Russes des derniers trois siècles, depuis le Czar Joan Wasiliewicz Groznyi jusqu'à l'Empereur Alexander II, 1547-1855. Atlas, 37 large embossed plates in metallic colors, separate in case (Nos. 1, 2, 6 and 14 missing). 331 pp. 4to, half calf. Leipsic, 1857.   2

710 Sharp, Thomas. A Catalogue of the Provincial Copper Coins, Tokens, etc., issued in Great Britain, Ireland, and the Colonies during the 18th and 19th centuries, in the collection of Sir George Chetwynd, Bart., Warwick. 280 pp. Folio, cloth. With Sir George's autograph. A rare and valuable work, but few copies issued. London, 1834.   1

711 Simon, James. Essay on Irish Coins and on the Currency of Foreign Moneys in Ireland, with Mr. Snelling's supplement. 188 pp., 12 plates. 4to, half calf. Dublin, 1810.   1

712 Stainsfield, C. W. Descriptive Catalogue of Australian Tradesmen's Tokens. 74 pp. and index. Several illustrations.
8vo, cloth. London, 1883. 1

713 Van Loon, Gerard. Histoire Metallique des XVII Provinces
des Pays Bas. 5 Vols. 2464 pp., profusely illustrated with
fine engravings throughout, singly and in groups. Index
and table of legends. A good copy of this valuable work.
Half calf, boards, folio. The Hague, 1732-37. 5

714 Pamphlets, Brochures, etc. Indian Coinage (Thomas) ; Jour-
nal Asiatique (1835) ; Le Roux, 1882, 1883 ; Low, Hard
Times Tokens, Morelos, Betts's Counterfeit Halfpence ;
Attinelli's Numisgraphics ; Dickinson's Plates, etc. 16

PRICED CATALOGUES OF AMERICAN COIN SALES.

715 1855 (2), 1858 (3), 1859 (7), 1860 (12), 1861 (2), 1862 (9). 35
716 1863 (8), 1864 (8, including the celebrated McCoy), 1865 (3),
1866 (5), 1867 (5, including the Mickley — first American
collection that came into prominence), 1869 (7). 36
717 1870 (6), 1871 (9), 1872 (4), 1873 (9), 1874 (8). 36
718 1875 (11), 1876 (15), 1877 (16). 42
719 1878 (18, including the Holland), 1879 (38, includes the
Schieffelin). 56
720 1880. 35
721 1881. 37
722 1882 (35), 1883 (5). 40
723 Bushnell, 1882, with and without plates, unpriced ; Warner,
1884, plates, printed prices, large 4to catalogues ; Parmelee,
bound copy with plates, unpriced, 1890. 4
724 Duplicates of priced catalogues (74), unpriced (32). 106
725 Dealer's Catalogues, Fixed Prices. Scott Stamp and Coin Co.,
Low, and Ponce de Leon, includes bound copy of Scott's
Copper Catalogue, 1890 ; also six foreign auction catalogues. 17

COIN HOLDERS.

Made of Card-board ⅛ inch in thickness, with circular holes of various sizes,
the bottom of which is lined with velvet paper. These are the same popular
holders as formerly sold by the Scott Stamp and Coin Co. and advertised in their
Catalogues of 1893-94.

726 ¾ in. hole (100), ⅞ in. (82), 1 in. (100), 1¼ in. (41), 1½ in. (100),
1¾ in. (68), 2 in. (59). 550

727    $\frac{3}{4}$ in. (91), $\frac{7}{8}$, 1 and $1\frac{1}{4}$ in. (100 each), $1\frac{1}{2}$ in. (34), $1\frac{3}{4}$ in. (100).   525
728    $\frac{3}{4}$, $\frac{7}{8}$ in. (200 each), 1, $1\frac{1}{4}$, $1\frac{1}{2}$, $1\frac{3}{4}$ and 2 in. (100 each).   900
729    $\frac{3}{4}$, $\frac{7}{8}$ in. (200 each), 1, $1\frac{1}{4}$, $1\frac{1}{2}$ and $1\frac{3}{4}$ in. (100 each).   800
730    $\frac{3}{4}$, $\frac{7}{8}$ in. (400 each), 1, $1\frac{1}{4}$ and $1\frac{1}{2}$ in. (200 each).   1400
731    $\frac{3}{4}$, $\frac{7}{8}$ in. (200 each), $1\frac{1}{4}$ in. (300), $1\frac{1}{2}$ in. (100).   800
732    $\frac{3}{4}$, $\frac{7}{8}$ in. (200 each), $1\frac{1}{4}$ in. (300).   700
733    $\frac{3}{4}$, $\frac{7}{8}$ in. (400 each), $1\frac{1}{4}$ in. (300).   1100
734    $\frac{7}{8}$ in. (400), $1\frac{1}{4}$ in. (300).   700

ADDENDUM.

735   1776 CONTINENTAL CURENCY Sun dial. ℞ 13 links and names of States. Pewter Dollar type of the Fugio Cent. Very fine and rare.   1

736   Gold. *Quarter Dols.* 1859 Octagonal, 8 stars. ℞ Value and date in wreath. Unc.   1

737   1870 13 stars. G date below. ℞ Value in wreath. Unc.   1

738   1871 Octagonal. Type as last. Uncirculated.   1

739   *Half Dols.* 1853 12 stars. ℞ " Half D. California Gold." Date within wreath. Unc.   1

740   1859 Octagonal, 11 stars. ℞ Value and date in wrth. Unc.   1

741   1872 Octagonal, 13 stars, date on obv. ℞ Value in wreath. Uncirculated.   1

742   *Dollars.* 1856 Dahlonega mint. Very fine. This piece, I believe, should rank in the highest class of rarities among the mint-marks found on Gold Dollars.   1

743   1863 Fine, very rare.   1

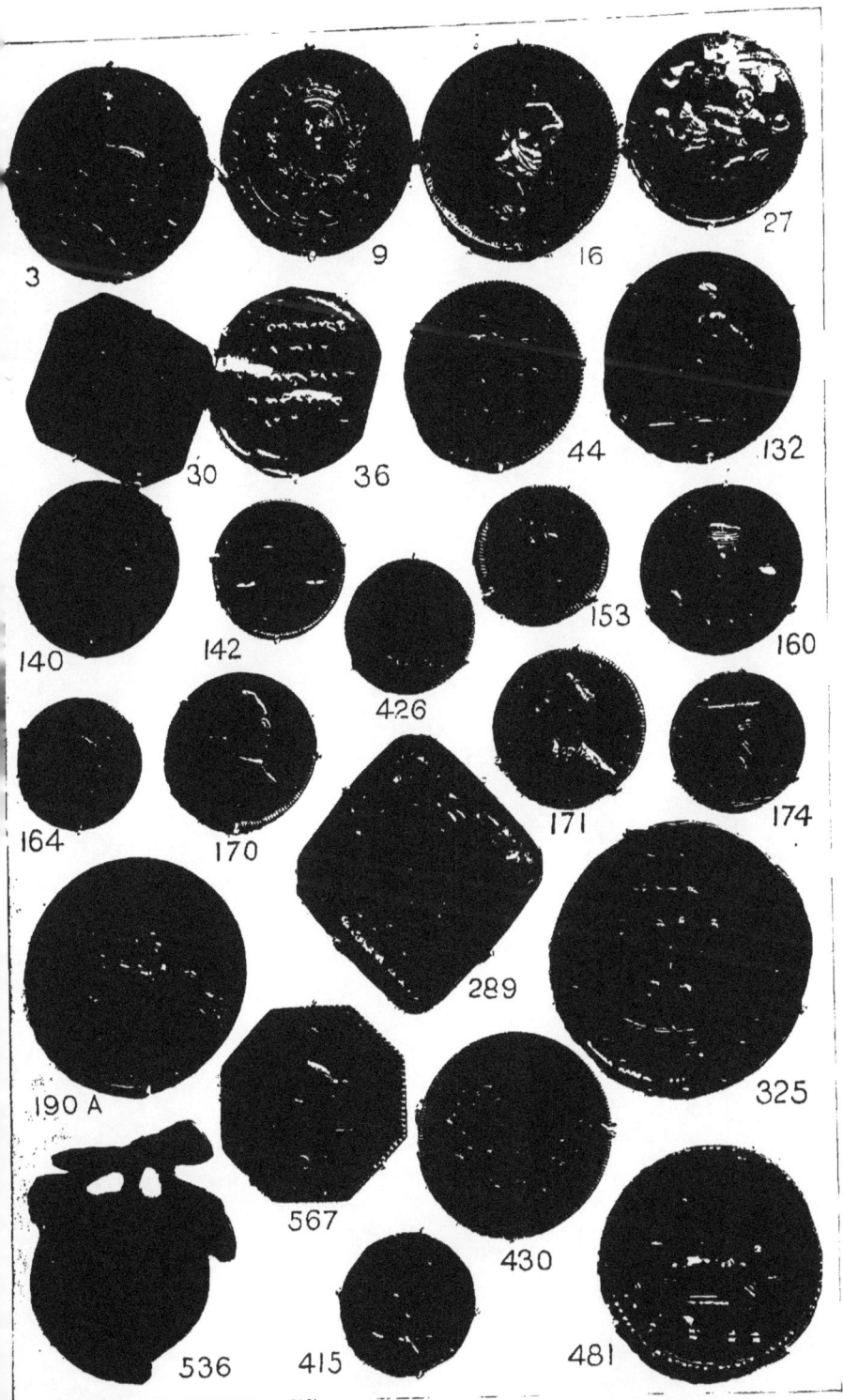

3   9   16   27

30   36   44   132

140   142   153   160

426   164   170   171   174

190 A   289   325

567   430

536   415   481

22

22

144

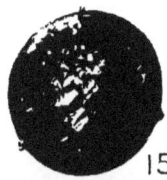

151

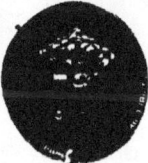

180

382

382

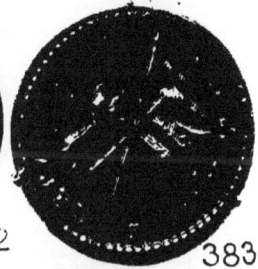

383

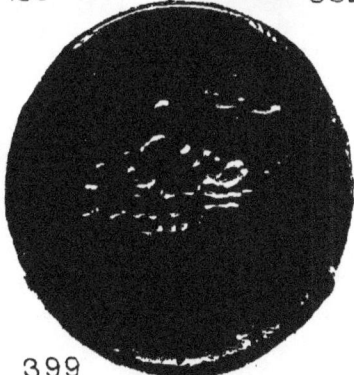

399

184

184

417

534

503

566

503

566

510

www.ingramcontent.com/pod-product-compliance
Lightning Source LLC
Chambersburg PA
CBHW021627270326
41931CB00008B/907